Acting Anthology
Volume 5

www.lamda.ac.uk

www.nickhernbooks.co.uk

Acting Anthology: Volume 5

First published in 2024 by the London Academy of Music and Dramatic Art,
155 Talgarth Road, London W14 9DA, United Kingdom, Tel: +44 (0)20 8834 0530,
www.lamda.ac.uk
and Nick Hern Books Limited, The Glasshouse, 49a Goldhawk Road, London W12 8QP,
United Kingdom, Tel: +44 (0)20 8749 4953, www.nickhernbooks.co.uk

Printed by TJ Books, Padstow, Cornwall
Cover, page and layout design by n9design.com

ISBN PB – 978-1-83904-328-4
ISBN EB – 978-1-78850-778-3

MIX
Paper | Supporting
responsible forestry
FSC
www.fsc.org   FSC® C013056

Contents

Foreword

I am delighted to introduce this stimulating collection of pieces from a range of exciting writers. Within these pages there are characters whom many young people will relate to, seeing themselves reflected in the words on the page. But there are also pieces that will challenge young people to see the world through someone else's eyes, catapulting them into different cultures, times and places in an instant.

These pieces present snapshots of compelling realities: you might find yourself in 1960s Tanzania fighting for women's rights (*The Maladies*) or you might choose to stay in today's world and advocate for the protection of our planet (*Heavy Weather*). You might discover the joy of dance in the daytime raves of 1990s British Asian culture (*Daytime Deewane*), or you might throw yourself into the fantastical landscape of daemons and alethiometers (*The Book of Dust*) – a world I am very familiar with! There are also some brilliant classical pieces, with funny, complex and memorable characters to choose from. Wherever you find yourself, allow these places to inspire you and the characters to get under your skin: they will teach you something new about being human.

A few things to ask yourself whilst rehearsing: what does my character want? How are they going to get it? If it's a monologue, who is my character speaking to? If it's a duologue, what does my character need from the other person? Don't be afraid to take the unconventional route – this is what will make the character *you*. Lastly and most importantly, make sure you enjoy yourself. If you want to shout a line one day and whisper it the next, go for it! Be playful. Be creative. Have fun.

Communicating the words, thoughts and feelings of a character in front of an audience offers lifelong benefits to young people. It can nurture imaginations, increase confidence, encourage empathy and even inspire professional careers. Many of the writings in this anthology explore life from a young person's perspective, with stories about young people, written for young people. Take ownership over these characters and allow them to spark your creativity and curiosity. They are yours to bring to life.

Ruth Wilson
LAMDA Graduate 2005

Introduction

This anthology has been carefully selected to offer Learners a broad range of material when taking their LAMDA Examinations. Throughout the collection, we engage with contemporary playwrights who write for the modern world, whilst looking back to classical material from writers whose work has stood the test of time.

We also feature new, original material from writers who have a connection to LAMDA, and it is a privilege to publish their work in this anthology. To LAMDA's Learners, we hope that this collection makes you excited to take your Examinations, whilst sparking your curiosity in different writers and the themes and topics they explore.

It is a pleasure to hand over to the likes of Sabrina Mahfouz, Jack Thorne, Bola Agbaje and Henrik Ibsen, and we hope you enjoy reading, studying and performing the works contained in this anthology.

Note on the Pieces

This anthology contains the set pieces for Learners taking LAMDA *Graded Examinations in Performance: Acting* from Grade 1 to Grade 5.

You may notice that in the case of certain selections, the spelling of some words may vary from piece to piece, representing either standard British or American spelling. To the best of our ability, LAMDA Examinations has selected pieces that are age-appropriate for Learners taking our Exams. However, some of the complete texts may contain themes, language, or terminology that Learners may find offensive or unsettling. Please bear this in mind when teaching younger Learners, and note that LAMDA Examinations does not endorse any discriminatory terminology that appears.

LAMDA Examinations is constantly exploring ways to make our anthologies as inclusive as possible. We work with the industry to create positive change and encourage conversations around inclusivity. When selecting pieces for Learners, we recommend approaching this with sensitivity and consideration of the themes of text and characters portrayed, particularly in relation to religion, race, gender and disability.

Thanks

LAMDA Examinations would like to thank all the authors, publishers and agents who made the development of this anthology possible. Special thanks are also due to Vinota Karunasaagarar, Julia Watson, David Aldred, Karen Roberts, Oleksandra Spiegler, Andy Pitts, Linda Macrow, Marcia Carr, Simeilia Hodge-Dallaway and Beyond The Canon, Matt Applewhite and Nick Hern Books.

Level 1 Acting: Grade 1 Solo

Is This A Fairytale?

Bea Webster

Jester is preparing to tell the audience a fairytale. For inspiration, Jester looks at the stories that have come before, but decides to invent a new narrative and ending. In this speech, Jester gets ready to tell their story.

JESTER: Hello! My name is Jester Blank. We are going to tell you a fairytale. But first, let's read the fairytales already out there and see what they are like!

(*Picks up a book and starts reading.*)

Once upon a time...

Once upon a time...

Once upon a time...

This one is about a Princess who wanted a Knight to come and save her.

EWWWWWWW.

This once is about a Princess who needed a true love's kiss to save her.

EWWWWWWW.

This one is about a Princess who wanted to find a Prince to marry her.

EWWWWWWWW!

Wait, hold up, hold up! What is wrong with that? Some Princesses want to marry a Prince. Some don't and that's okay. I mean, one day I want to get married!

But it's straight away, without even getting to know the Prince!

What if the Prince is not a nice person?

Oh. Yeah! I never thought about that before!

EWWWWWWW.

Why are all fairytales the same? They all end the same way.

I feel like this doesn't represent all Princesses well at all. I mean, what if the Princess wants to marry another Princess?

What if the Prince wants to marry another Prince?

What if the Princess doesn't need a Knight and can fight for themselves?

What if the Princess is a they? Like, I mean you can be a Prince or a Princess. But what if you don't feel like a Princess or a Prince? Do we need a new term for that? Like... erm... Princette?

Should we invent a new fairytale?

Should we invent the BEST FAIRYTALE EVER?

Wait... Look! There! We have a Princess up in this tower.

It's like in the books!

Do we need to tell her she doesn't need a Knight to save her if she doesn't want to?

That maybe she doesn't need saving at all?

Does that mean we can change the story?

We should come up with a different ending!

(*All Jesters agree with each other!*)

Right! Are we all ready?

Let's do this!

Let's start with the Princess!

Hey Princess!

HEY PRINCESS!

PRINCESS!

PRINCESS!

Cheese and Pickle

Rosa Hesmondhalgh

Robin's Grandpa used to work in Darwen, Lancashire. In this speech, Robin recalls a summer when they were staying with their Grandpa. Robin's Grandpa wants to go walking, and although Robin is initially reluctant, they are soon won over by the view from Darwen Hill.

ROBIN: My Grandpa used to work in a factory in a little town in Lancashire called Darwen. In Darwen there is a tower called Darwen Tower, and every lunch time my Grandpa would walk up Darwen Hill and go and eat his sandwiches – cheese and pickle, every day – under the shadow of the big Darwen Tower. It was built about twenty-five years before he was even born, and waaaaaay before he knew he was gonna be my Grandpa. When he retired, he kept walking up there – *every single day.* Last summer, when I was staying with Grandpa, he came into the living room with his hat on and put his hands on his hips.

'Right little'un. It's a wonderful day for walking and walking is what we'll do.'

I said no at first because my cousins said they might come and pick me up and take me shopping at the Trafford Centre. Also I was watching a TV programme about how crisps were made and I was interested to know how they got them so crisp-y. But he wasn't having any of it.

'Before we had the Trafford Centre we had fresh air and walks and views for miles.'

So off we went. We drove to the bottom of the hill, and parked next to the factory where he used to work, and then started up the hill. I don't like walking up hill really.

'Grandpa, I don't like walking up hill, really.'

He pointed, silently, at his calves. I nodded. Very strong calves. I knew he was telling me if I want strong legs like him I should walk up more hills. We got to the top and he got out the sandwiches he'd packed. Cheese and pickle for him, as usual, and one with just ham for me.

Then we looked.

I could see for *miles.*

You could see all the way to Blackpool Tower. The sun was making everything look...

Really beautiful. I suppose.

'So, you used to come here every day?' I asked Grandpa. 'Didn't you ever get bored of the same thing?'

Grandpa looked at his sandwich. 'No.'

And then I looked at Blackpool Tower, and the hills, and my sandwich, and my Grandpa, and I realised: some things just don't get boring.

'Shall we come back tomorrow, Grandpa?'

The Raven

Hannah Lavery

Alex is alone in their room during the pandemic. Since starting secondary school, they have drifted from their friend Fran, and their Mum has become more and more unwell. In this speech, Alex describes their life at home.

ALEX: Headphones on.

Music loud.

As loud as I can stand.

Lights out.

Door shut.

And still, I can hear her...

I can still hear her –

Alex! Alex!

Leave me alone.

Will you just leave me alone!

I throw my phone at the door.

Make a dent.

Break the phone,

and now it's all her,

it's her, all the time...

Alex! Alex!

Leave me alone, Mum!

Please just leave me alone!

Truth is...

She's not always been like this...

I am not sure if I know how to describe it.

She's not herself, that's what my dad says, and that's true, she's not like herself – she's not how I like to think of her.

When Dad's out on shift, she says she's always been this way.

That's not true, I say.

That's not true, Mum.

It's just the lockdown, right?

She was fine before... Mostly things just got too much for her...

Fran's mum used to look after me, when Mum was working and when she got ill. But now, it's all about keeping Fran safe, no room for waifs and strays now, not with the virus – aye, right. Not since her precious wee child... I mean, they shouldn't be prying – right? My mum, my business. I don't need them. We're fine.

My mum is very special, that's what Fran's mum said, but she has never been this ill, not for this long. She doesn't seem that special anymore and it's doing my head in.

(*A moment passes.*)

I wish I hadn't broken my phone.

Act 1, Scene 2, 'Alex'

Edward II

Christopher Marlowe, adapted by LAMDA

Prince Edward is the son of King Edward the Second, who recently died, leaving Prince Edward to be crowned King at the age of fourteen. As Prince Edward learns of his father's death, he is informed that Mortimer and Queen Isabella – his mother – are suspected of murder. Prince Edward orders Mortimer's death, and in this speech he sends his mother to the tower.

PRINCE EDWARD: Forbid me not to weep; he was my father;
And had you lov'd him half so well as I,
You could not bear his death thus patiently:
But you, I fear, conspir'd with Mortimer.
Mother, you are suspected for his death
And therefore we commit you to the Tower,
Till further trial may be made thereof.
If you be guilty, though I be your son,
Think not to find me slack or pitiful.
Away with her! her words enforce these tears,
And I shall pity her, if she speak again.

(*Enter First Lord with the head of Mortimer.*)

Go fetch my father's hearse, where it shall lie;
And bring my funeral robes. Accursed head,
Could I have rul'd thee then, as I do now,
Thou hadst not hatch'd this monstrous treachery! –
Here comes the hearse: help me to mourn, my lords.

(*Enter Attendants with the hearse and funeral robes.*)

Sweet father, here unto thy murder'd ghost
I offer up this wicked traitor's head;
And let these tears, distilling from mine eyes,
Be witness of my grief and innocency.

Act 5, Scene 6

The Letter

Trish Cooke

*The Windrush generation is a term used to refer to people who arrived in the UK
from Caribbean countries between 1948 and 1971. In this speech, it's May 15th,
1962, and nine-year-old Clare has been sent for to travel from the Caribbean, to
join her mother and father in the UK.*

CLARE: I am excited about the trip to Englan' but I thought me, and Grannie
and Millie were all going to go together – but the letter I read from Mammy to
Grannie says different...

(*She reads.*)

Dear Mama,

We are sending the money to pay for Clare's passage to England. Make all the
arrangements. Cecil and myself look forward to seeing our eldest girl.

'But Grannie, I can't go by myself' I say, and Grannie says, 'Your Mammy sen' for
you. You must go. Millie will soon follow.' 'But I don't want to go to Englan'!' I say.
But she doesn't listen.

My Mammy and Daddy are strangers to me. They go to Englan' when I was
small. They don't know me, and I don't know them, so why must I leave my
Grannie and my sister, to go to them?

(*Pleading.*) 'Grannie, I want you and Millie to come too. Let's all go together!' I
say. But she explains how Mammy and Daddy can't afford to send for all of us to
travel together. She say they will send for Millie later.

I beg 'Please Grannie don't send me to Englan'! Let me stay home, in Dominica! I
will die without you, Grannie!'

But Grannie tell me I have to go. She say I have to be with my Mammy and
Daddy in a new place. A new home. I must go to an English school. She tell me I
have to forget about Dominica. But I will never forget! Never!

(*Pause.*)

Millie looks at me different now. She say if it was her, she would never leave me. I tell her I don't have a choice. 'I hate you!' she say. I know she doesn't mean it, but it still hurts. My eyes are pricking me, the tears are burning but I keep my eyes open wide, so the tears don't fall. I want to be brave like Grannie tell me I should be.

'I will write to you every day' I say to Millie, and she calls me a liar. She tells me I will forget her as soon as I reach England and go to all the fancy places. She tells me I will become an English girl. I want to let her know that I will never change, but I don't know how.

Androcles and the Lion

George Bernard Shaw, adapted by LAMDA

Androcles is walking down a jungle path and comes across a lion. Androcles is initially frightened, but then realises that the lion has a thorn stuck in its paw. Androcles decides to help and befriend the wounded lion.

ANDROCLES: Meggy: run. Run for your life. If I take my eye off him, it's all up.

(*The lion holds up his wounded paw and flaps it piteously before Androcles.*)

Oh, he's lame, poor old chap! He's got a thorn in his paw. A frightfully big thorn. (*Full of sympathy.*) Oh, poor old man! Did um get an awful thorn into um's tootsums wootsums?

(*The lion responds by moans of self-pity.*)

Yes, yes, yes, yes, yes. Now, now (*Taking the paw in his hand.*) um is not to bite and not to scratch, not even if it hurts a very, very little. Now make velvet paws. That's right.

(*He pulls gingerly at the thorn. The lion, with an angry yell of pain, jerks back his paw so abruptly that Androcles is thrown on his back.*)

Steadeee! One more little pull and it will be all over. Just one little, little, leetle pull; and then um will live happily ever after.

(*He gives the thorn another pull. The lion roars and snaps his jaws with a terrifying clash.*)

Oh, mustn't frighten um's good kind doctor, um's affectionate nursey. That didn't hurt at all: not a bit. Just one more. Just to show how the brave big lion can bear pain, not like the little crybaby man. Oopsh!

(*The thorn comes out. The lion yells with pain, and shakes his paw wildly.*)

That's it! (*Holding up the thorn.*) Now it's out. Now lick um's paw to take away the nasty inflammation. See?

(*He licks his own hand. The lion nods intelligently and licks his paw industriously.*)

Clever little liony-piony! Understands um's dear old friend Andy Wandy.

(*The lion licks his face.*)

Yes, kissums Andy Wandy.

(*The lion, wagging his tail violently, rises on his hind legs and approaches to embrace Androcles, who makes a wry face.*)

Velvet paws! Velvet paws!

(*The lion draws in his claws.*) That's right.

(*Androcles approaches the lion with his arms wide.*)

Prologue

Off the Grid

David Lane

Kelly has an older brother called Connor. In this speech, five-year-old Kelly is at school at the 'making table', doing crafts. As Kelly completes her activities, she tells her new friend a story about her family dynamic.

KELLY: I'm Kelly

(*Phonetically.*) *K – E – L – L – Y*

You're new so you can sit here

And you can use the makin' table

But not the things I'm usin' til I've stopped usin' them

I'm makin' this

It's a cake

(*KELLY beams.*)

I'm actually a superhero

And also I was born in a golden egg like for real in an *actual* golden egg

Because –

It's a secret story don't tell and then we can be bestests

– Um

Once upon a time

Once upon a time

This is a story ready

There was a Mummy eagle and a Daddy eagle who had golden eggs

Who knew that if a Mummy went to hunt for food

The Daddy should stay in the nest

And if a Daddy went to hunt for food

The Mummy should stay in the nest

They should never leave golden eggs on their own

'Cos two bad things would happen if they did

First the Mummy and Daddy would vanish

Into two piles of fluffy feathers

And second

The chicks in the golden eggs

They'd be born as people

Tiny human-people-eaglet-thingies in a nest

Who wouldn't be able to fly or catch mice or see tiny things from far away

Because they had no-one to teach them

But the *big* problem in the story

Was that *all* the food in birdland was bein' eaten by bigger birds like...

Condors

And even though the Mummy and Daddy knew about the two bad things

They knew their eaglets would be really really hungry when they hatched

So they left the nest together to get food

And *poof* they disappeared

Don't use that felt tip I need a yellow one.

Chapter 2, 'Why Eagles Never Leave Their Eggs'

Little Violet and the Angel

Philip Osment

Gabriel is a young angel who has just arrived in heaven. Gabriel's first task is to look after an orphaned girl as she grows up with her adoptive parents. In this speech, Gabriel tries to figure out who she is.

GABRIEL: Gabriel's the name.
I'm an angel you know.
Like my wings?
Bit small, aren't they?
They're not proper ones.
I haven't earned my proper ones yet.
I've just arrived you see.
Apparently I used to live down there.

(*Gabriel looks down.*)

Whoa!
I hate heights.

(*Gabriel looks down again.*)

Whoooahooooah.
Long way down isn't it?
Funny thing is
I don't remember a thing about being down there.
No-one ever does.
I just woke up surrounded by all these clouds and celestial beings.

His name's Gabriel too.
My boss.
But he's the big cheese.
He's what you call an archangel.
You should see the wings on him.
They're massive!
I'm just a common angel.
In the scheme of things
I'm not much higher than a cherub.
In fact he was quite upset,
The other Gabriel, I mean,
I suppose he didn't want to be sharing his name with somebody as low down the pecking order as me.

Anyway
I haven't got time to dawdle talking to you.
Got work to do,
Places to go,
People to see.
I'm looking for a little girl.
I'm supposed to be her guardian angel.
I have to watch over her.
It's my first job.
He said,
If I do it well,
Then I might get wings like his.
Perhaps you've seen her. Have you?
He gave me a description
My boss,
The other Gabriel.
Hang on.

(*Gabriel gets out a piece of paper and reads.*)

Two eyes...

(*Gabriel looks at the audience.*)

Hmmm.

(*Gabriel reads the paper again.*)

A nose...

(*Gabriel looks at the audience.*)

Mmmm.

(*Reads the paper.*)

A mouth...

(*Gabriel looks at the audience.*)

Mmmmm. Giggles when she's tickled.

You!

Scene 2, 'Heaven'

It Makes You Wonder

Nick Teed

*Ashley tells a friend about the events of a Christmas Day that they will
never forget.*

ASHLEY: It was that time on a Christmas Day when the kitchen is just a mass
of piled up dirty plates and dishes and pans. I'd been sending texts... all about
presents and money and food. So, I'm stood at the kitchen window and mum's
rushing around like she does, with her party hat on, searching for a tin of salmon
to give to grandma to take home. I'd been allowed one small glass of sparkling
wine and it was there on the worktop. I thought it might have gone flat so I held it
up. I was looking for bubbles...

How can I explain it? A flickering orange glow on the side of the glass... does
that make sense? I just moved my eyes a fraction past the glass... it only took
a second to focus on Mrs Medlock's bungalow across the street. There were
flames in her kitchen window!

When they burst the door down, they started coughing straight away but they
ran in. We waited in the street. They got her out, over dad's shoulder. She was
unconscious... pale. *You've* seen Molly, her cat out in the street haven't you? I
thought, '*She might be in there somewhere*'. So, I looked in and she was there in
the hallway. Dad was yelling at me to stay away but I grabbed her and ran for it...

I saved a scared cat. Big deal. Dad and uncle Jack saved Mrs Medlock, *that's*
praise worthy. But people keep expecting me to be all happy and excited
because '*we were all so brave*'...

I *can't* be happy about it because... well, as I grabbed Molly, I looked in the living
room. There was a small table with a couple of cards on it and a tiny Christmas
tree with fairy lights. The dining table was set near the window. Don't know what
she was having for dinner... that was burning in the kitchen... but there was *one*
dinner plate, *one* bowl, *one* Christmas cracker... What would *you* think if you saw
that? How sweet? How sad? All those years, all those Christmas Days since her
husband died she'd been on her own while we partied across the street. Makes
you wonder, doesn't it? How many other Mrs Medlock's are out there; keeping
going all on their own?

Wendy & Peter Pan

Ella Hickson, adapted from the novel by **J. M. Barrie**

Tootles, whose nickname is 'Little Tootles', is in Neverland. Prior to this speech, Tootles and the Lost Boys have been told that Pirates are hunting them. Unarmed, Tootles ran to fetch a bow and arrow, but this means that Tootles has been separated from the group. In this speech, Tootles is hunting a crocodile and a bird. Aiming his bow at the sky, Tootles accidentally shoots Wendy.

TOOTLES: (*With his eyes closed*) I can shoot the crocodile – I know I can if only I'm – (*Opens eyes and the Crocodile has gone. Gives up, downcast.*) brave. (*Stops suddenly and stares at the forest floor, where Skylights has been despatched.*) There's... (*Tests it.*) blood on the ground. Boys? Boys! What if they've been taken – what if it's my fault – what if –

(*Tink appears - as a small, bright light.*)

Tink! You're back! Have you seen the boys? Did you see what happened – there's blood? Look – there's – a bird? No – listen – Peter wants me to shoot a bird? Where? It's a very big white bird. No, but really I have to find the boys – 'brave'? Peter said I was brave? I have to shoot it because I'm the bravest? Me?

(*Tootles looks up - then aims his bow and arrow up at the sky.*)

You're right – you're right, Tink. If Peter wants it doing then I'm the man for the job.

(*Tootles aims his arrow at the bird. Tootles shoots - the arrow soars high. Tink's light flies off.*)

I hit it! I hit it, Tink! Go and tell Peter, Tink – tell Peter I hit the bird! I am the bravest! Tell Peter, tell Peter I hit the –

(*Wendy comes tumbling to the ground and lands in a heap. Tootles looks at her.*)

Tink? This doesn't look like a bird. Tink? Where have you gone?

(*Tootles goes close to Wendy and inspects her.*)

I think I might have made a mistake.

(Pause. Tootles steps back in horror. Tootles sees the Lost Boys approaching and covers the bird up as best he can.)

Boys! You're all right, I thought there'd been a skirmish – there was blood on the floor.

(Tootles steps in front of Wendy.)

What are you looking at?

(Tootles, again, tries to stand in front of Wendy.)

What – this? It's a white bird – it's a big white bird – that's all it is – Tink said that Peter said that I should shoot it and I did – I shot it and hit it because I'm brave, okay – so there. You should cheer like you do when Nibs hits a bird, go on – cheer.

Act 2, Scene 3

Level 1 Acting: Grade 1 Duologue

The Fir Tree

Hannah Khalil

The Fir Tree, whose nickname is the 'Little Fir Tree', and Child are in the woods during Spring. At the start of this scene, a hare jumps over the Fir Tree's branches, leaving the Fir Tree feeling disgruntled. The Fir Tree is then approached by a Child, who wants to sit and read their book. The Fir Tree is curious about books, but the Child does not have the heart to tell the Fir Tree where books come from.

(*A hare jumps over the Fir Tree and speeds off.*)

FIR TREE: Every morning. Why does Hare have to do that every morning?

CHILD: Morning, Fir Tree – do you mind if I sit here next to you and read this book?

(*Child has a book which says on the cover 'The Stories of Hans Christian Anderson'.*)

FIR TREE: Sure.

(*The Child begins to read, engrossed.*)

(*Beat.*)

FIR TREE: What's a book?

(*The Child looks up slightly annoyed – they were getting into their story.*)

CHILD: This – this is a book.

FIR TREE: Oh. Right.

(*The Child returns to reading.*)

(*Beat.*)

FIR TREE: What's it for?

(*The Child looks up slightly more annoyed – they were getting into their story.*)

CHILD: Reading. Obviously.

FIR TREE: I see.

(*The Child waits a moment to see if the Fir Tree has any further questions then, when none emerge, returns to reading.*)

(*Beat.*)

FIR TREE: And what exactly is reading?

(*The Child sighs and puts their book aside – they are clearly not going to get any reading done with this inquisitive tree.*)

CHILD: Well, it's sort of magic.

FIR TREE: Magic? How – what does it do? Can it make a hare disappear?

CHILD: Oh no, not that kind of magic.

FIR TREE: Shame.

CHILD: It can transport you.

FIR TREE: Like the trucks that sometimes come to the forest?

CHILD: Um – noo – I don't think so... you see this book can take you anywhere, any time. It can magic you out of this wood to anywhere you like. Without ever moving.

FIR TREE: Oh how wonderful! Where does that book go?

CHILD: To the palace of a great Emperor in China who falls in love with a Nightingale's song!

FIR TREE: You're so lucky! Where do you get such a thing?
And what is it made of?

CHILD: Well, a story is made of thoughts and ideas and hopes and dreams... and those are put into words – lots of words placed together in interesting ways.

FIR TREE: I see.

CHILD: And there's usually a moral.

FIR TREE: What's that?

CHILD: A sort of meaning or lesson, something you can learn about the world or yourself.

FIR TREE: You're very clever. And this book – what is it made of?

CHILD: Pages that are bound together.

FIR TREE: And pages – what are they made of?

CHILD: Oh. Um, pages are...

(*Beat.*)

I'm – um – I'm not sure what pages are made from...

(*Beat.*)

FIR TREE: Well, I think books sound brilliant. I'm sick of being stuck in this boring old wood.

CHILD: What do you mean? It's beautiful here. Bluebells. And bees. Ladybirds and leaves.

FIR TREE: If you like that sort of thing. But it's always the same: a circle of branches, three-hundred-and-sixty degrees of soil, sky above, ground below and – I want adventure.

I want to know what the other trees know.
Go where the other trees go.
Where do they go?

(*A bell rings in the distance.*)

CHILD: Crikey – I'm late. Again. I'll get into such trouble! Goodbye, Fir Tree – see you another day!

FIR TREE: I want to know what the other trees know.
Go where the other trees go.
Where do they go?

Part 1, 'Spring'

The Skin You're In

Rosa Hesmondhalgh

New Banana (NB) and Old Banana (OB) meet in a fruit bowl. The New Banana is positive about their future, having just arrived from the supermarket; however, the Old Banana is resigned to their fate as a decaying fruit. That's until the New Banana finds Old Banana a new purpose.

(*A fruit bowl. An old, sad, slightly bruised banana is decaying in the corner. A brand new, green banana arrives from the supermarket.*)

NB: It's even better than I imagined!

OB: Watch it buddy. You'll bruise yourself if you're not careful.

NB: Oh! Sorry. I'm just excited to be here. I've been sat in that supermarket for a whole day and then I got put in the trolley and – boop – got scanned through the self checkout machine and – woop – here I am!

OB: I was like you once. Green. Excited. Certain of my future.

NB: Are you okay? You're looking a little worse for wear.

OB: You're foolish, young one. People don't wear bananas. They eat them. Or at least that's what I thought.

NB: You're... you're a banana? Like me?

OB: Yep. I'm just a really old banana.

NB: How old are you?

OB: About three weeks. Do you know anyone that old?

NB: ...No one. What was it like... back then?

OB: Well, when I was yellow and perfect, I arrived here. Things were looking good for me. But, the family went on holiday and I guess they didn't want to take any snacks. I was left here. And now they've come back and done a whole new shop and brought you back.

NB: You could still get eaten. I'm underripe! Not ready for eating right now.

OB: I'm past the point of enjoyment.

NB: You're really old, sure, but also wise! You must have seen *so much.*

OB: Oh yes. I'm still thinking about the great Fruit Fly Infestation of a week and a half ago.

NB: See! You can teach me so much about what life is like in a fruit bowl. All I remember is the supermarket — what happened before then?

OB: We were on a tree.

NB: A what?

OB: Big thing, branches, lots of leaves. Where we came from.

NB: Wow.

OB: Our life's purpose? To be eaten. And look at me. I'm destined for the compost bin.

NB: Well, a note on the fridge over there says the compost collection isn't until Thursday, so.

OB: You can read?

NB: Sure, my shelf was next to the magazine rack in the supermarket. I got really good at crosswords. Wait. There's something else stuck to the fridge. Let me read – oh! Old Banana, this is a recipe... for banana bread!

OB: Banana bread?

NB: It calls for overripe bananas!

OB: That's me!

NB: See? Overripe, not old. You have purpose, and meaning, just maybe not the one you originally thought. Maybe I'll be banana bread too.

OB: For such a green banana, you're pretty wise yourself.

Ella and Buttons Make Their Own Party
Trish Cooke

Ella's mean stepsisters have told Ella that she cannot go to the Ball with them. They have torn up her invitation, ruined her dress and damaged the portrait of her deceased mother. In this scene, Buttons tries to cheer Ella up.

(Kitchen. There is a table with a tablecloth on it. Ella is alone looking sad. Buttons runs on and sees Ella.)

BUTTONS: Ella! (*Disappointed.*) You're not coming to the ball?

ELLA: No Buttons, I don't want to go anywhere with *them!* I hate them! I hate them! They've ruined my dress, torn up my invitation and... (*Showing him her mother's damaged portrait.*) Look what they've done to mum's portrait!

BUTTONS: I'm gonna tell your dad!

ELLA: No Buttons, let dad enjoy himself. The less he knows the better. No point both of us being miserable.

BUTTONS: (*Feeling sorry for her.*) Come on, you don't need to go to that stupid ball. We can have a party right here.

ELLA: A party? Here? How?

BUTTONS: Get that tablecloth!

(Ella hesitates then decides to play along with Buttons. She gets the tablecloth and Buttons drapes it on her. Together they make a makeshift dress out of it. Buttons then arranges the chairs to look like a carriage.)

BUTTONS: Your carriage awaits, Ma'am.

ELLA: (*Playing along.*) Thank you, kind sir.

(Ella gets onto the 'carriage' and Buttons pretends they are moving along as they journey to the palace.)

BUTTONS: Such a beautiful moonlit night and the softest warm breeze caresses your skin.

ELLA: (*Playing along.*) Feels wonderful.

(*He stops the carriage.*)

BUTTONS: Now here we are, we've arrived. Time for some dancing.

ELLA: But where are all the other guests?

BUTTONS: (*Calls.*) Tom! Dick! Harry!

(*Three puppet mice scurry across the floor and join them.*)

BUTTONS: Time to party!

(*Buttons taps a beat, and the three puppet mice begin to dance. Ella is amused. She dances with them.*)

BUTTONS: It's good to see you dancing again Ella…

ELLA: (*Happy.*) This is the best party I've ever been to in my life!

(*Buttons watches in awe as Ella continues to dance – the plan has worked. It is as if Ella is in another world as she dances.*)

ELLA: (*Dancing.*) Thanks Buttons. Hey, you better go or they'll be wondering where you are.

(*Buttons watches her dance for a moment, then he blows her a kiss and leaves.*)

Adventures of Snow Black and Rose Red

Valerie Mason-John

The Anansi legend originated in Ghana, West Africa, with the Ashanti tribe. In Akan, the word Anansi means spider, making him one of the most popular animal tricksters of West African mythology. In this scene, two nine-year-old friends have been captured by Anansi. Snow Black (African Caribbean) and Rose Red (Asian) are convinced that they have been eaten alive and are determined to escape.

(The sound of a cellar door slams shut, and the key turning echoes out loud. The two girls scramble from the sack.)

SNOW BLACK: Where are we?

ROSE RED: I think we're in the big man's belly.

SNOW BLACK: Me too – it so dark and damp in here

ROSE RED: Let's see if we can find his belly button.

SNOW BLACK: Why?

ROSE RED: Because my mummy says the belly button is what pulled me out of her tummy.

SNOW BLACK: In that case we need to find a stork.

ROSE RED: Why?

SNOW BLACK: Because my mummy says the stork brought me as a present from her tummy.

ROSE RED: Okay then I look for the big man's belly / button.

SNOW BLACK: And I'll look for the stork – but we must walk on tip toes.

ROSE RED: Why?

SNOW BLACK: Shush can't you hear him snoring.

ROSE RED: I'm scared.

SNOW BLACK: I am too.

ROSE RED: Let's hold hands.

SNOW BLACK: Quick.

(*Snow Black and Rose Red begin looking for a way out.*)

ROSE RED: I think the big man is waking up.

SNOW BLACK: But he can't be he's still snoring.

ROSE RED: Can't you see how light it's getting.

SNOW BLACK: I think I've found his mouth.

ROSE RED: Where?

SNOW BLACK: Over there, look I can see some trees.

ROSE RED: Let's see if we can swim out of his mouth.

SNOW BLACK: Ouch.

ROSE RED: What's the matter?

SNOW BLACK: His mouth isn't open, and I bumped my head.

(*Rose Red falls about laughing.*)

SNOW BLACK: It's not funny, and shush you will wake him up.

ROSE RED: Look over here, you bumped your head on a window, we're lost in somebody's attic I think.

SNOW BLACK: Are we dreaming, please tell me we're dreaming. You promised to meet me at the river last night before you went to bed.

ROSE RED: I don't think it is a dream, my mummy told me not to meet you at the river in my dream, just in case I wet myself.

SNOW BLACK: If it's not a dream where are we? I want to go home.

ROSE RED: Me too.

SNOW BLACK: We must find our way home.

Scene 3

Oliver Twist

Anya Reiss, adapted from the novel by **Charles Dickens**

After an altercation with Noah Claypole, nine-year-old Oliver escapes and runs away to London. He is spotted by Jack Dawkins, whose nickname is 'the Artful Dodger'. In this scene, Jack approaches Oliver, who initially confuses him for Noah Claypole having grown sleep-deprived and confused from his travels. Jack warns Oliver of the traps and dangers of London, and then encourages Oliver to follow him to safety.

JACK DAWKINS: Oi Oi. What's the story here then?

(*Oliver sees Jack who laughs and approaches, Oliver is distressed.*)

OLIVER: Not you!

JACK DAWKINS: Not me?

OLIVER: What?

JACK DAWKINS: What?

(*Beat.*)

OLIVER: (*Confused.*) You hate me

JACK DAWKINS: I hate you? Do I? Is that right?

OLIVER: You insulted my mother

JACK DAWKINS: Now why would I do a thing like that?

OLIVER: I don't understand. I... Who are you?

JACK DAWKINS: – My name is Jack. Jack Dawkins. Now can I ask you again, what's the story here, governor?

OLIVER: (*Resigned.*) I don't know what's going on anymore

JACK DAWKINS: Do any of us

OLIVER: I'm, I'm on my way to London

JACK DAWKINS: London? Well you made it. You're here

(*Oliver looks around – it doesn't seem like anything's changed.*)

JACK DAWKINS: Not like you expected?

(*Oliver shakes his head.*)

JACK DAWKINS: We should be careful though, traps round here

OLIVER: Traps?

JACK DAWKINS: Police

OLIVER: I haven't done anything

JACK DAWKINS: Think that matters. How green are you?

OLIVER: Green?

JACK DAWKINS: You're joking right?

(*Oliver looks unsure.*)

JACK DAWKINS: Innocent. Naive. Like a child

OLIVER: I am a child

JACK DAWKINS: So am I but I ain't a fool

OLIVER: You aren't a child!

JACK DAWKINS: What am I then? A sparrow?

OLIVER: No I just mean you seem... older

(*Beat.*)

JACK DAWKINS: Maybe I'm just wiser country boy

(*Oliver is confused, Jack moves away.*)

JACK DAWKINS: Come on then

OLIVER: What?

JACK DAWKINS: Got no money, got nowhere to stay, got no family too I bet. Am I right?

OLIVER: Yes

JACK DAWKINS: I am right. And this ain't looking that much like London? The one you imagined. The one you heard of. From all the stories

(*Oliver shakes his head.*)

JACK DAWKINS: Then I got just the gentleman who would like to meet you.

(*Jack grins and claps twice; smoke, noise, colour and a sea of handkerchiefs hanging from above appear.*)

JACK DAWKINS: Welcome to London.

Part 1

Little Red and Big Blue's Deal

Trish Cooke

Little Red Riding Hood begs her sister, Big Blue Bossy Boots, to give her a chance to prove to their mum that she can be trusted to go through the woods, and take the broth to Grannie's house.

(Outside Little Red Riding Hood's house.)

LITTLE RED RIDING HOOD: It's not fair! I want to bring the broth to Grannie's, but Mum won't let me. Mum's always going on about how she has to do everything round the house and how she could do with the help, but she doesn't let me do anything.

(Upset.) Why won't Mum trust me?

(We hear a rustle in the bushes.)

BIG BLUE BOSSY BOOTS: Pssssssssssst! Hey sis!

(Little Red Riding Hood looks around and sees Big Blue Bossy Boots coming out of her hiding place in the bushes.)

BIG BLUE BOSSY BOOTS: Little Red!

LITTLE RED RIDING HOOD: Stop calling me that! I aint little! If you didn't have those boots on, you would be shorter than me...!

BIG BLUE BOSSY BOOTS: *(Interrupts.)* Sharrap! Respec' ya elders!

LITTLE RED RIDING HOOD: Thought Mum sent you to bring Grannie her broth anyway, what you come back for?

BIG BLUE BOSSY BOOTS: *(Looking around, making sure Mum has gone.)* Was just thinking... Maybe Mum's being a bit unfair... Felt sorry for yer...

LITTLE RED RIDING HOOD: You did?

BIG BLUE BOSSY BOOTS: Yup. Thought I'd help you out... Give you a chance to prove to Mum that you can do a job without messing up... So, here's the broth. Take it to Grannie's...

LITTLE RED RIDING HOOD: (*Surprised, about to grab the broth.*) Thanks Big Blue!

BIG BLUE BOSSY BOOTS: (*Pulling the broth away.*) ...But I dunno if I can trust you not to mess up... I dunno, I dunno...

LITTLE RED RIDING HOOD: Gimme it! I won't mess up! I promise.

BIG BLUE BOSSY BOOTS: Ok. (*Changes her mind*) Nah... you know what...? (*Deliberating*) I don't think you're ready... (*Walking away*) Forget it.

LITTLE RED RIDING HOOD: Please Big Blue! I won't mess up!

BIG BLUE BOSSY BOOTS: You sure?

LITTLE RED RIDING HOOD: I'm sure!

BIG BLUE BOSSY BOOTS: (*Takes her time to think about it.*) Ok. Here you go.

(*Gives Little Red Riding Hood the broth.*) Take this broth to Grannie's and be back for six thirty or else!

LITTLE RED RIDING HOOD: Wicked! Thanks Blue. (*About to go then stops.*) What are you gonna do?

BIG BLUE BOSSY BOOTS: (*Showing off, clicking her fingers diva style.*) I got somewhere to go! – *big people business!*

(*As Big Blue Bossy Boots leaves, Little Red Riding Hood jumps for joy, pleased with herself.*)

LITTLE RED RIDING HOOD: Yes!!!

Like Lennon
Rosa Hesmondhalgh

As Cam rushes to leave for school, Harri daydreams about being the lead singer of a band, with Cam as the guitarist or drummer. Initially, Cam resists Harri's fantasies, but is eventually moved and won over by Harri's words.

(*Cam is rushing to leave the house, Harri is lounging on the sofa, deep in thought.*)

CAM: Ok Harri, we need to leave right this second.

HARRI: If we were in a band, would I be the lead singer, or would you be the lead singer, do you think?

CAM: Huh? No – no time for that, we need to go.

HARRI: I think you have a slightly better singing voice but I have more stage presence. I think I have dance moves and an exciting look.

CAM: Honestly we need to walk through that door in two minutes or – wait. An exciting look?

HARRI: Yes.

CAM: That haircut? You'd call that an exciting look?

HARRI: What's wrong with my haircut?

CAM: The hair, mainly.

HARRI: My Mum says I look like John Lennon, when I've got my glasses on.

CAM: Go on. Put 'em on.

(*They do.*)

CAM: I'm not seeing it. You look like your Mum.

HARRI: Well, my Mum looks a bit like John Lennon. Speaking of which, he was a great leader of a band, so if I look like him, my point is proven.

CAM: I don't know how we've got onto this, but we really do need to leave. We're going to be late, as usual.

HARRI: Musicians are famously late.

CAM: Yes, but we're not musicians.

HARRI: Not with that attitude. What about: I'm the lead singer, but you get to have like, a fun guitar solo?

CAM: I don't play guitar.

HARRI: Drums then.

CAM: We're not in a band! This argument has no logical basis. Can we please go?

HARRI: Can I please be the lead singer?

CAM: Oh, *fine*. Fine! If you insist, and if it will get you out of the door quicker, then sure. Be the lead singer.

HARRI: Oh, this is such a surprise.

CAM: Of a band that doesn't exist.

HARRI: I didn't even have a speech prepared.

CAM: I'm leaving. You can stay here and write your speech.

HARRI: I'd like to thank my Mum, for giving birth to the next John Lennon, and my best friend and bandmate Cam for letting me be the lead –

CAM: You're thanking me?

HARRI: Of course.

(*Cam blushes.*)

CAM: That's – oh. That's lovely.

HARRI: Thank you to the talented Cam for all the support.

CAM: Keep going.

HARRI: Cam's going to do an amazing guitar solo.

CAM: Yes.

HARRI: And it doesn't matter if that makes us late for school.

CAM: Ah, who cares. We're musicians! We're famously late.

Peer Gynt

Henrik Ibsen, adapted by LAMDA

Peer Gynt is the son of the peasant widow Åse. He has been banished from his home and is roaming the mountains. He comes across the Green-Clad One, a woman wearing green claiming to be the daughter of the troll mountain King. They decide that they'd be a perfect match for marriage.

(A hillside, wooded with great soughing trees. Stars are gleaming through the leaves; birds are singing in the treetops. The Green-Clad One is crossing the hillside; Peer Gynt follows her, with all sorts of lover-like antics.)

GREEN-CLAD ONE: (*Stops and turns round.*) Is it true?

PEER GYNT: (*Drawing his finger across his throat.*) As true as my name is Peer; – as true as that you are a lovely woman!
Will you have me? You'll see what a fine man I'll be.

GREEN-CLAD ONE: You're a king's son?

PEER GYNT: Yes.

GREEN-CLAD ONE: I'm the Dovre-King's daughter.

PEER GYNT: Are you? See there, now, how well that fits in!

GREEN-CLAD ONE: Deep in the Ronde has father his palace.

PEER GYNT: My mother's is bigger, or much I'm mistaken.

GREEN-CLAD ONE: Do you know my father? His name is King Brose.

PEER GYNT: Do you know my mother? Her name is Queen Åse.

GREEN-CLAD ONE: When my father is angry the mountains are riven.

PEER GYNT: They reel when my mother by chance falls a-scolding.

GREEN-CLAD ONE: My father can kick e'en the loftiest rooftree.

PEER GYNT: My mother can ride through the rapidest river.

GREEN-CLAD ONE: Have you other garments besides those rags?

PEER GYNT: Ho, you should just see my Sunday clothes!

GREEN-CLAD ONE: My week-day gown is of gold and silk.

PEER GYNT: It looks to me like tow and straws.

GREEN-CLAD ONE: Ay, there is one thing you must remember: –
this is the Ronde-folk's use and wont:
all our possessions have twofold form.
When you shall come to my father's hall,
it well may chance that you're on the point
of thinking you stand in a dismal moraine.

PEER GYNT: Well now, with us it's precisely the same.
Our gold will seem to you litter and trash!
And you'll think, mayhap, every glittering pane
is nought but a bunch of old stockings and clouts.

GREEN-CLAD ONE: Black it seems white, and ugly seems fair.

PEER GYNT: Big it seems little, and dirty seems clean.

GREEN-CLAD ONE: Ay, Peer, now I see that we fit, you and I!

PEER GYNT: Like the leg and the trouser, the hair and the comb.

GREEN-CLAD ONE: Bridal-steed! Bridal-steed! bridal-steed mine!

(*A gigantic pig comes running in with a rope's end for a bridle and an old
sack for a saddle. Peer Gynt vaults on its back and seats the Green-Clad One in
front of him.*)

PEER GYNT: Hark-away! Through the Ronde-gate gallop we in!
Gee-up, gee-up, my courser fine!

GREEN-CLAD ONE: (*Tenderly.*) Ah, but lately I wandered and moped and pined.
One never can tell what may happen to one!

Act 2, Scene 5

Recycling Mayhem
Kirsten Charters

Jessie has been told off by their parents for putting the recycling in the incorrect bin. Frustrated, Jessie tries to put all the recycling into the non-recycling bin, but then gets dragged through the bin into Recycling Land. There, Jessie meets The Bin who teaches them the importance of recycling.

JESSIE: My parents are having another go at me! I've put something in the wrong bin, again!

You see this box of chocolates? It needs separating – plastic lid in this bin, cardboard box in this bin and this chocolate I dropped needs to go into the compost, wrappers in the soft plastics – it's no wonder I get confused! I've had enough, I'm starting a revolt! I am going to be rebellious and put it all in here... the non-recycling.

(*Jessie puts the rubbish in and feels a tug on the arm.*)

Owwww!

THE BIN: Hold on tightttttttt!

(*Jessie falls through the bin.*)

Welcome to Recycling Land Jessie!

JESSIE: That hurt!

THE BIN: Sorry didn't mean to pull on you so hard!

JESSIE: Who are you?

THE BIN: I'm a bin.

JESSIE: What kind of a smelly old bin are you?

THE BIN: I'm a 120 Litre Outdoor Heritage Bin, one of the best around. I come in a range of colours too.

JESSIE: (*Sarcastically.*) How impressive.

THE BIN: Now don't be cheeky with me, that's what got you into this mess in the first place.

(*The Bin starts to open The Bin Code Book.*)

Now, under section 2.4A of the recycling bin code, I hereby conclude that you did break bin law by placing mixed items in the non-recycling bin at precisely 3.04pm on Thursday 5th June, how do you plead?

JESSIE: Guilty as charged.

THE BIN: I like your honesty!

JESSIE: The punishment?

THE BIN: See that pile of rubbish over there, it needs sorting into the correct bins. Well off you go, you broke bin law you know.

JESSIE: I can't believe I'm taking orders from a bin.

(*Jessie starts to sort out the rubbish.*)

THE BIN: Come on Jessie, where's your enthusiasm for the environment?

JESSIE: I don't care!

THE BIN: YOU DON'T WHAT?

JESSIE: Recycling is a waste of time.

THE BIN: Oh I'm in so much shock my bin lid nearly fell off. Tell me what's your favourite animal?

JESSIE: Easy, a dolphin.

THE BIN: Look at that plastic bottle in your hand? By recycling it, we can help to ensure it doesn't reach the ocean and ruin natural habitats for animals like dolphins.

JESSIE: Oh right, I didn't realise. Actually, I have a reusable drinks bottle at home that I never use.

(*The Bin starts to frantically open The Bin Code Book.*)

THE BIN: Oh goodness, I should caution you under section 7.2B of the recycling bin code for not reusing your bottle... but I'll let you off this time.

JESSIE: I guess I have been a bit lazy.

THE BIN: And selfish...

JESSIE: Alright, no need to get personal, can't believe I'm getting grief off a bin.

THE BIN: We want to use these products again so they are not wasted. Remember this phrase Jessie: Reuse, Reduce, Recycle.

JESSIE: Wow look at this...a retro games controller! I reckon I could fix this.

THE BIN: Then take it with you and reuse.

JESSIE: Cheers Bin.

THE BIN: It's time for you to return, I do hope you won't break the bin code again.

JESSIE: I promise I won't.

THE BIN: Take my bin hand and I'll send you back to your world.

JESSIE: Have you sanitised it?

THE BIN: Yes.

JESSIE: I'm going to need a bath when I get back. Or a shower? Uses less water?

THE BIN: Ah, my work here is done.

(*Jessie takes The Bin's hand and lands on the floor at home and notices a chocolate.*)

JESSIE: Oooo I missed a chocolate!

(*Jessie unwraps and eats the chocolate, then throws the wrapper to the floor and exits. Jessie returns and picks it up and places it into the soft plastics bin.*)

Just kidding!

Peter Pan Goes Wrong

Henry Lewis, Jonathan Sayer and **Henry Shields**

Cornley Polytechnic Drama Society are putting on a production of Peter Pan. They have a history of things going wrong in the plays that they produce, but they're hopeful that the Christmas production will be more successful. Competing for the spotlight, Chris and Robert introduce the play to the audience.

CHRIS: Good evening, ladies and gentlemen.

ROBERT: Boys and girls.

CHRIS: And welcome to the Cornley Polytechnic Drama Society's Christmas production of J. M. Barrie's classic...

ROBERT: *Peter Pan*!

CHRIS: Please allow me to introduce myself; I am Chris, the director.

ROBERT: And I'm Robert, the co-director.

CHRIS: Assistant director. We're hugely excited to present *Peter Pan* as this year we've managed to secure a much larger budget than usual thanks to a sizeable donation from the uncle of one of our cast members, Max. This generous cash injection has meant that tonight's production will certainly outshine last year's rather underfunded Christmas show that Robert directed: *Jack and the Bean.*

ROBERT: But we are optimistic for tonight's pantomime...

CHRIS: It's not a pantomime, Robert, it's a traditional Christmas vignette.

ROBERT: Oh no it isn't.

CHRIS: ...Hahaha. It's true we've had several productions where the vision just hadn't been fully realised.

ROBERT: In one of Chris's productions, due to an ill-timed haircut Rapunzel had to be imprisoned in a bungalow.

CHRIS: Indeed that was almost as bad as when Robert insisted on using a real

cat in his production of *Puss in Boots*, which became known among the society as *Puss Who Was Occasionally in Boots, But Often Refused to Wear His Boots, and Pooed in Them.*

ROBERT: But this year everyone has come together and we even have my young niece Lucy to play the Lost Boy Tootles.

CHRIS: Absolutely, who we are sure will overcome her chronic stage fright this evening. We have taken every possible precaution to ensure the smooth running of the show.

ROBERT: Including a top of the range radio headset for our actor Dennis to ensure he remembers his lines correctly.

CHRIS: Don't tell them about the headset.

ROBERT: Well, it's true, Chris, he doesn't know a single line. It's certainly undermined past productions; like when he played the title role in *Oliver!* In the workhouse scene he got up, walked over to Mr Bumble and said 'Please sir, I'm full'.

CHRIS: So it is with huge excitement that we present tonight's production. With no further ado, please put your hands together for...

ROBERT: (*Comes in too early.*) Peter P–

CHRIS: J. M. Barrie's...

ROBERT: (*Too early again.*) Peter–

CHRIS: Christmas classic...

BOTH: *Peter Pan*!

Act 1, Scene 1

Level 1 Acting: Grade 2 Solo

When This Is Over

Allegresse Kabuya with **Ned Glasier, Sadeysa Greenaway-Bailey** and **Company Three**

A group of teenagers unite to tell their stories, from childhood to the present day. After experiencing the global Coronavirus pandemic, Allegresse reflects on her youth and the problems she sees in the world.

ALLEGRESSE: It felt like there were more problems than ever.

Problems on top of problems.

Covid, George Floyd, Donald Trump, cancel culture, burning the Amazon, Boris Johnson, Liz Truss, World War Three, heatwaves, food prices, rents, benefit cuts, Andrew Tate, heatwaves, fracking, old white men, monkeypox, gangs, Mahsa Amini, extinction, Sarah Everard, racism, that boy who got stabbed outside Highbury Fields, GCSEs, pressure, nuclear bombs, famine, parents, wildfires, Russia, Jeffrey Dahmer, teachers, floods, abortion, Chris Kaba, fossil fuels, mental health, dictatorships.

When they talked to their parents about how it felt like everything was in chaos they said:

Allegresse, be careful, the world is a wicked place, trust me I know how the world works – when you grow up you'll understand.

It was like they were being fed fairytales, stories of the world, placebos. Like they were hypnotised, that the world was gonna be okay but they realised, it wasn't okay.

It was like everyone was pretending even though they knew, even though they talked about it – trying to live in the moment but they couldn't because they had to keep accepting, keep it stepping, more stuff got added, choices got changed, another decision, another problem – all these problems and still no solution.

It felt like no one wanted to imagine how the future could be different.

But then they realised that it was just because they were young then. That all the problems had always been there, that it was scary then too, just no one had told them about it. Yet.

'Problems'

Robin Hood

Laura Dockrill, adapted from the novel by **Howard Pyle**

Robin returns home and finds that the Sheriff of Nottingham is starving the people of Sherwood Forest. The courageous Robin vows to stand up for the suffering people. In this speech, Robin speaks to the 'Merry Many', a group of outlaws who steal from rich people and give to the poor.

ROBIN: RIGHT! There appears to be some confusion in our camp. Let me clarify. As it appears some of us here need reminding... Our home has been confiscated by a tyrant. Since King Richard the Lionheart has left for his crusade we are under the thumb, lock and key of a merciless and barbaric man. The Sheriff has no empathy and there's no reasoning with him. Please do not EVER think for a second that living in the extremities of today's ruthless tax and penalty charges that there is wiggle room for selfishness. Forget what you had before. Because that is not life outside of these woods anymore.

We live for now! We are The Merry Many and we fight for now! We can help! We are young, fit and able. And wanted, yes. We are wanted but there is freedom in that too. I mean, we're already in deep trouble – how much deeper can we get? We can help those the same way we would like to help ourselves and each other. We take from those that have enough to spare, we share and we reward ourselves for our hard work with food and wine and the company of our friends. The things that money can't buy.

The forest pays us, richly, beautifully, with the golden warmth of the smiling orange sun every morning, the clean clear fresh spring of the stream that washes us, our skin, our clothes and quenches our thirst. The way the trees and bushes provide us with shelter, beds, places to hide, to keep safe. The fruits from branches that are sweet and ripe that you can pluck from your bedside. The ground gives us wheat. Corn. The air is ours, the harmony of birdsong that lullabies us to sleep, the pearl torch of a moon that protects us each and every night. That keeps us sound. Fearless. Brave. This forest gives us everything.

And if you don't like that, Will, you don't have to stick with us. You can go back to town where your hands will be tied and you'll be captured and strung up. Gutted. Then, you'll see how much you think you deserve.

Act 1, Scene 3, 'The Real Robin'

Twitch

Rosa Hesmondhalgh

Kai is on their way to a Royal Society for the Protection of Birds (RSPB) reserve with their Mum and Weird Wendy. They can't think of anything worse. But when Kai catches sight of a rare type of owl, their feelings change.

KAI: I'm in the car to an RSPB reserve in the furthest corner of absolute nowhere, on a Saturday, with my Mum and her friend Weird Wendy, to go and look at birds. When I should be at my best friend Sammy's water park party. My Mum's insistence on making me have a bad day is borderline *criminal.* I don't care about birds, I care about water slides.

What?

I'm not talking to anyone, Mum. I'm talking to... the universe. About how unfair this is. I'm telling the cars and the trees and the big sign just there that says 'RSPB: GIVING NATURE A HOME' – we're here, are we? Great.

Big forest. Big pond – no waterslides – some pigeons. *Great.*

If I wanted to see pigeons, I'd open my window at home and see that massive scary one that looks like an eagle and leaves its poo everywhere and coos so loudly it wakes me up before my alarm. Coooooooooo. Like that. I hate pigeons.

So Mum, you've dragged me away from my best friend's party to my mortal enemy's dwelling place. What's first? Walk around the pond? Look through some binoculars? Fight a pigeon? An owl? There's a special, rare type of owl. It's apparently hiding in a tree, no one has ever seen it: you're hoping to see it today.

Let me say that again.

No one has ever seen it.
You're hoping to see it.

I don't mean to rain on your RSPB reserve, but, the odds of – where are you going? You and Weird Wendy can go to the cafe, I'll wait here. If they have cake, could you – Mum? Hello?

If I was at Jo's birthday party, I'd be having cake, post-waterslide. Jo's Mum is literally a professional baker.

That pigeon's watching me. I bet it's been sent to spy on me by the one on my windowsill. It's massive, and I can see its one gross eye, yellow. Yellow? Pigeons' eyes aren't yellow are they? Hang on. It just *hooted.* Not a weird coo – a hoot! I want a better look. It looks straight out of a David Attenborough documentary. Oh it's – *OH!*

MUM. Put that decaf Americano down and C'MERE. I've seen THE OWL!! And *bring your binoculars.*

See?

All the RSPB volunteers are running to have a look. They're patting me on the back, congratulating me for spotting it. They've brought me cake. This isn't so bad. Maybe they could put some waterslides in their lake – I might come back next week.

The Wish Collector

Oladipo Agboluaje

Sam is in his bedroom playing 'Lunar Wars', his favourite video game. In this speech, Sam demonstrates his skill for the game, but is meanwhile troubled by the reality of his home life. Sam wishes that his family could be happy once again.

SAM: Shoot-em-up, RPG
Upgrade weapon
Level three
Watch me race
Into battle
Power up
Win the game
Online fame
Restart game

I'm playing 'Lunar Wars'. Win a battle and your moon waxes brighter. I'm the best in my class. 'Lunar Wars 2' is just out. Mum's promised to get it for me if my grades improve. Dad promised he'd buy me a Game Player. Mum said he wouldn't because he's so stingy. Dad called Mum a nag. Then we all laughed. I wish no one gets them before I do. Got to keep my crown in the playground, you know. Now if I can just reach Level Ten one more time...

(Game over.)

(Jumps up in frustration.) Oh! Nearly, nearly.

(Restart game.)

What I like about 'Lunar Wars' is that you can start all over again. Fail and just press 'restart'. You're always in control even though you haven't got the latest Game Player and some nerd called Chris is stealing your crown!

(Sam continues playing.)

For days I'd get lost in a world of battles and heroes. That must have been when it started. We used to sit at the table for dinner. That was in the good old days before I reached Level Ten. Those were the good days. I wish they'd come back.

(Sam stops playing. Looks up at the sky.)

I'd give up all the moons I've won if Dad comes back home. We'll all be happy like before. I'll go and see a romantic movie with them and we'll cry into our hankies. Dad will say 'I didn't cry', and Mum will say 'Yes you did!' and she'll ask me 'was your Dad blubbering like a baby?' And Dad will say, 'He couldn't see me. He was crying more than you.'

This Massive Universe

Hannah Kennedy

When Juno is abducted by aliens and shown the wonders of the universe, their mind is blown. Back on Earth, Juno struggles to adjust to normal life. In this speech, Juno explains their feelings to their best friend, who is worried about their behaviour.

JUNO: I know I've been acting weird! I know! I'm not... I'm not stupid. Okay? I know sometimes I seem like I'm mentally on another planet. And I know you probably want to know why. You're my best friend. I get it. If you were acting like this, I would want to know why too. But... I don't think you would believe me if I did tell you.

And don't say you would! Because this is a big one, this is a massive one. This one is, honestly, genuinely off the scale. And I'm not just saying that, I promise. I'm not just being vague for the fun of it to create some sort of air of mystery around me because, truthfully, and I really, really mean this, if I thought you would believe me, I would tell you.

Come on. Don't look at me like that. Don't you roll your eyes at me! I have been friends with you since we were six years old, do you really think I'd be trying to pull the wool over your eyes?

Fine! Fine. Fine, I'll tell you. But you can't tell anyone.

Okay. So... You know how I disappeared for a couple of weeks over the summer? And everyone thought I'd been kidnapped. And then I turned up in the woods just a couple of miles outside of town? And I told everyone I couldn't remember where I went? Well, I do remember. And I was kidnapped. I was abducted. I was abducted by aliens.

And yeah, I know that sounds... well, it sounds... it sounds like I've completely let my imagination run away, but it's the truth. I was abducted by aliens, and the things I saw... They, these aliens, they showed me the universe. They showed me how amazing and different and scary and... massive this universe is. Things that I don't think I will ever truly understand.

And then they brought me home. Back here. To my normal life, with my normal family, where I go to my normal school, and I hang out with my normal friends.

And nobody understands, nobody gets it. I know so much, and I feel so, so alone. I look up at the night sky and see all those stars. And I feel so tiny.

So, I'm sorry if I seem a little out of sorts. I'm trying to... I don't know. I'm trying to find meaning again when I'm so insignificant, and this universe is so big.

Through the Looking-Glass

Lewis Carroll, adapted by LAMDA

As Alice shows her cat the Looking-Glass House, she is amazed when the glass they're looking through melts away. Alice finds herself in the Looking-Glass room and is excited to discover what lies within it.

ALICE: First, there's the room you can see through the glass – that's just the same as our drawing room, only things go the other way. And then there's the bit behind the fireplace – I do wish I could see *that* bit! I wonder whether they've a fire in the winter: you never can tell, you know, unless our fire smokes, and then the smoke comes up in that room too – but that may be only pretence, just to make it look as if they had a fire. The books are something like our books, only the words go the wrong way; I know that, because I've held up one of our books to the glass, and then they hold up one in the other room.

How would you like to live in the Looking-Glass House, Kitty? I wonder if they'd give you milk in there? But oh, Kitty! Now we come to the passage. You can just see a little *peep* of the passage in Looking-Glass House, if you leave the door of our drawing-room wide open: and it's very like our passage as far as you can see, only you know it may be quite different on beyond.

Oh, Kitty! How nice it would be if we could only get through into Looking-Glass House! I'm sure it's got such beautiful things in it! Let's pretend there's a way of getting through into it, somehow, Kitty. Let's pretend the glass has got all soft like gauze, so that we can get through.

(*The glass begins to melt away.*)

Why, it's turning into a sort of mist now! Wait... it should be easy enough to just... (*Alice starts to climb through the glass*) climb through... (*Alice jumps lightly down into the Looking-Glass room.*)

Wow.

(*Alice looks around.*)

Oh! The pictures – they're alive! And this clock has the face of a little old man. And here are the Red King and the Red Queen. And there are the White King and the White Queen sitting on the edge of the shovel – and here are two castles walking arm in arm.

(*Alice peers at the two castles.*)

I don't think they can hear me. I'm nearly sure they can't see me. I feel somehow as if I were invisible. I've got to see what the rest of the house is like!

Chapter 1, 'Looking Glass-House'

A Husband for Mum

Trish Cooke

Eleven-year-old Callum wants to find a husband for his single mum, and he thinks he's the perfect person to find her match, as he knows her better than anyone.

CALLUM: Ever seen a beautiful woman and wonder why she's single? My Mum's single. Single yes, but I guess she's not really on her own, cos she's got me. Young, carefree, witty, charming, an ideal companion…

What I'm worried about is later, when all those girls won't be able to keep their hands off me. Don't want her crying in her coffee and pining for some male company then, cos then I'll be too busy being grown up!

The thing is Mum could have any man, but she doesn't want *any* man. Since she split up with Dad, she's convinced herself there's only one perfect match for everyone. She actually believes her soul mate's out there, somewhere. She believes in it so strongly, I think she's probably met him already, in a past life or something, but she let him pass her by.

Now me, I believe you've got to go after what you want in life. Things don't just fall on your lap out of the blue… Least that was what I thought before last week…

(*Beat.*)

We were coming home from shopping when I was quizzing Mum about stuff… you know personal stuff. I said to Mum –

'So, if you had a choice, of any man in the whole world, who would you choose?' And she just looks at me and laughs. 'Come on, your ideal man?' I say, and she says, 'OK, Brad Pitt'. I mean really? Brad Pitt's a Hollywood star and he's got millions of women after him. Dad's good looking and look where *that* got her!

So, I say, 'Maybe you should go for someone less good looking.' And before I can finish what I am saying it happens! This Beetle car, looks like Herbie from that old film, *Herbie Rides Again*, but it's red with a blue and white stripe on the bonnet, it comes speeding towards us and the driver slams on the breaks, just in time and the goofiest man I've ever seen comes out, and calls out Mum's name… And I think to myself… now this could be him.

At First I Was Afraid… (I Was Petrified!)
Douglas Maxwell

Libra is a Fairy Godcarer. In this speech, they appear before Cleo, who struggles with anxiety. Libra reassures Cleo that it's okay to be worried sometimes.

LIBRA: It's fine to be worried. Worrying means that you're imagining *consequences*, yeah? It means you have something at *stake* in your own life. People who don't worry don't care, and who cares about people who don't care? D'ye know what I mean?

You've just got to keep those worries in their place. They're not the main course… they're a spice. A little bit of zest to sprinkle over your life here and there for a bit of oomph. After all, you can't eat a great big bowl of paprika, can you now? No. So keep the worries in a tiny little jar at the back of your mind cupboard where they belong.

(*Cleo is still petrified.*)

But okay… I'm not gonna lie: sometimes things do go wrong. Accidents happen. Mistakes are made. Stuff doesn't always turn out the way you want it to. Sometimes you fail. Sometimes you get ill. It's a crazy world… it's a *maddening* world… but it is *no way* an awful world. Because for all the problems humankind has caused, humankind will find a solution. Trust me. Humankind is *astonishingly* good at finding solutions to things. In fact it's our most attractive trait. And yeah, it would be quite nice if humankind didn't cause all the problems in the first place, but what ye gonna do? And guess who's finding the solutions to all those problems?

(*Cleo doesn't know.*)

Worriers. But nothing'll get done if all the worriers stay in their bedrooms will it? Nah, we need the worriers out there on the street: putting their hands up… volunteering… making suggestions… starting clubs… taking risks… ignoring the haters… climbing that wall and screaming at the tops of their lungs.

(*Seriously.*) Do you believe me, Cleo? Can you feel… in your heart… that you… *you*… have the power to make this a better world? Can you be brave? Can you inspire?

(*Cleo nods.*)

Scene 3

King Henry V

William Shakespeare, adapted by LAMDA

King Henry V has ascended the English throne and is invading France. During the assault on Harfleur, Boy observes the criminal behaviour of Bardolph, Pistol and Nym. In this speech, Boy reflects on their pickpocketing schemes and decides to remove himself from their company.

BOY: As young as I am, I have observed these three swashers. I am boy to them all three, but all they three, though they would serve me, could not be man to me, for indeed three such antics do not amount to a man.

For Bardolph, he is white-livered and red-faced, by the means whereof 'a faces it out but fights not. For Pistol, he hath a killing tongue and a quiet sword, by the means whereof a breaks words and keeps whole weapons. For Nym, he hath heard that men of few words are the best men, and therefore he scorns to say his prayers lest 'a should be thought a coward: but his few bad words are matched with as few good deeds, for 'a never broke any man's head but his own, and that was against a post when he was drunk. They will steal anything, and call it purchase.

I must leave them, and seek some better service; their villainy goes against my weak stomach, and therefore I must cast it up.

Act 3, Scene 2

Come to Where I'm From

Sarah McDonald-Hughes

Ten-year-old Lily lives in Manchester. Her dad is a builder who recently lost his job. His final project was building a tower until it was the tallest building in Manchester. Every Saturday, Lily's dad picks her up and takes her for a day out. This week, Lily and her dad stop off at a canal where they reflect on the changes in their hometown.

LILY: By the Palace Theatre, me dad jumps up and rings the bell and we're getting off the bus. Dad takes us down some steps onto a canal. There's crisp bags and cans and that in the water, but there's some ducks an' all, and a shopping trolley sticking up which is pretty mint, really.

I follow me dad along the side of the canal. It's alright down here, nice really, quiet – apart from a few dogs and runners and bikes and that. Then me dad stops and he stares up at a building. It's a car park, I think, an underground one, with flats on the top.

'See this, Lil?' He seems a bit angry all of a sudden and I don't know what we're looking at. 'Probably the most important place this town has ever had. Tony Wilson'd be turning in his grave.' 'What is it, Dad?' 'The Haçienda, Lil. Where I met your mum. Best club in the world.' It's started raining. My dad starts walking up and down the canal, bouncing around on the side of the water. I don't know what he's talking about. 'Everywhere you look now it's flats and Tesco Metro and it's as if none of this ever happened. And I don't want no part of it. I don't want to build all these hard faced, heartless buildings in the place of things that were real and important and true.'

It's proper chucking it down now but me dad sits down, right there on the path. 'I just thought... that I could have one last stab at it. At being who I want to be and doing something big, and with a bit of meaning, d'you know what I mean?' Then the worst thing ever happens. My dad looks up at the sky and the rain's falling on him and I see that it's mixing with the wet that's already running out of his eyes.

Suddenly there's no bikes or dogs or runners and it's just me and my dad and the canal and the car park that used to be the best club in the world. I crawl onto my dad's knee. My dad wipes his face with the back of his hand.

'So what about you? Do you think I'm a loser an' all?'

'No,' I say, cos I don't. 'You built the tower dad. Look, Dad. There it is.'

I look into the black canal, all shiny like oil. And then – it's there. Stretching high above everything, reflected in the water all bright and shiny and special. And I know it'll always be there. Watching me.

Level 1 Acting: Grade 2 Duologue

The Book of Dust – La Belle Sauvage

Bryony Lavery, adapted from the novel by **Philip Pullman**

Malcolm and Alice are protecting newborn Lyra Belacqua who is being hunted by authorities, including the Consistorial Court of Discipline (CCD). Before this scene, twelve-year-old Malcolm and fifteen-year-old Alice have just had an altercation with Gerard Bonneville and ended up shooting Bonneville's daemon. Malcolm and Alice also steal Bonneville's rucksack which contains his research on 'dust'. Although they momentarily escape with Lyra, the CCD are close behind them.

(*They are in the canoe. Malcolm's teeth are chattering alarmingly. Dusk.*)

MALCOLM: My teeth won't stop chattering!

ALICE: It's *shock,* Malcolm.
You probably need a little cry...

MALCOLM: I'm just *cold* okay? (*He's not.*)

ALICE: Okay.

MALCOLM: Okay. (*But he starts shaking with trying to stop his teeth chattering.*)

ALICE: If you want a little cry, I won't tell on you.

(*Lyra starts crying.*)

Look! Lyra's crying.

MALCOLM: I'm *not* crying.

(*Beat.*)

Did we kill him?

(*Silence until...*)

ALICE: Probably.

(*Beat.*)

I hope so.

MALCOLM: He was bleeding *a lot*.

(*Beat.*)

I think there's an artery there in his leg.
And that daemon...

ALICE: I shot her. (*She allows the thought in.*)
He can't live if I've shot *her* surely. (*It's a dreadful, terrifying thought.*)

MALCOLM: No.

ALICE: Anyway, they won't be able to move. Neither of them.

MALCOLM: Hope so.

(*Beat. The thought builds.*)

Every time I try to do something safe for Lyra,
I just make it more dangerous for her!
I just murdered somebody!

(*And bursts into tears. Lyra cries too. Then...*)

ALICE: So did I!

(*Alice cries too.*)

MALCOLM: Sorry!

(*They cry it out separately until...*)

ALICE: Alright. Stop. Enough crying! What's done is done! We got a baby to look after!

(*Beat.*)

Mal.

MALCOLM: What?

ALICE: You done good.

(*Silence for a bit until...*)

MALCOLM: I'm *so starving!*

ALICE: Me too!
(*This makes them cry-laugh.*)
I'm gonna open that that hyena's rucksack... see if there's something to eat.

MALCOLM: I could *kill* for a biscuit!

ALICE: S'not funny!
What the bleeding hell is this?

(*She's found a small box. She opens it. An alethiometer. Malcolm takes it.*)

MALCOLM: It's an alethiometer!
Dr Relf says there's only six of these in the whole world!
He shouldn't have one... he must have stolen it.

ALICE: I wish he'd stolen some *food!*

MALCOLM: (*He's examining it as closely as he did the acorn.*)
I wonder if you can get inside it somehow... see how it works.

ALICE: There's just that thing...

MALCOLM: Alethiometer...

ALICE: And loads of papers –
(*Reads.*) 'An analysis of some philosophical implications of the Rusakov field by

Gerard Bonneville, PhD.' It's full of equations and signs... here, Professor, you can probably understand it.

(*She hands them to Malcolm.*)

MALCOLM: I doubt it! (*Scans the papers*) Must be his research...
(*Reads*) 'We conscious beings make Dust. We renew it all the time, by thinking, by reflecting, by gaining wisdom and passing it on.' We should take this to a college or something... we better keep it dry.

(*Searchlights strafe the area. They hear the CCD calling out.*)

ALICE: Oh no! CCD!

MALCOLM: We're sitting ducks out here!

(*They get the into the bank, take Lyra, and start running, trying to dodge the searchlights.*)

Act 2, Scene 7, 'Canoe'

The Wind in the Willows

Kenneth Grahame, adapted by LAMDA

Rat, whose nickname is 'Ratty', and Mole are in the Wild Wood when it begins to snow, and they completely lose their way. On the hunt for shelter, Mole trips over a doorscraper, which prompts Rat to discover a doormat and consequently, a door.

MOLE: Ahhhhhh! I can't see a thing!

RAT: We have got to keep going.

MOLE: My legs – the snow, it's too deep!

RAT: Look, Mole!

MOLE: What?

RAT: There's a sort of dell down there in front of us.

MOLE: Where? I can't see anything.

RAT: *There!* Where the ground seems all hilly and humpy and hummocky. We'll make our way down to that, and try to find some sort of shelter, a cave or a hole with a dry floor to it, out of the snow and the wind. Quickly!

(*They wade through the snow and reach the dell, where Mole suddenly trips and falls forward on their face.*)

MOLE: O, my leg. O, my poor shin!

RAT: Poor old Mole! You don't seem to be having much luck today, do you?

MOLE: I must have tripped over a hidden branch or a stump. O my! O my!

RAT: It's a very clean cut. That was never done by a branch or a stump. Looks as if it was made by a sharp edge of something metal. Funny!

MOLE: Well, never mind what done it. It hurts just the same.

(*Rat starts to busily scrape the snow.*)

MOLE: O, come on, Rat!

RAT: Hooray!

MOLE: What?

RAT: Hooray-oo-ray-oo-ray-oo-ray!

MOLE: What *have* you found, Ratty?

RAT: Come and see!

MOLE: A doorscraper! Well, what of it? Why dance jigs round a doorscraper?

RAT: But don't you see what it means?

MOLE: It *means* that some very careless and forgetful person has left their doorscraper lying about in the middle of the Wild Wood, *just* where it's *sure* to trip *everybody* up.

RAT: O dear! O dear! Here, stop arguing and come and scrape!

(*Rat scrapes at the ground and comes across a doormat.*)

RAT: Look, what did I tell you?

MOLE: Absolutely nothing whatsoever.

RAT: Mole, look – there's a doormat here.

MOLE: Can we eat a doormat? Or sleep under a doormat? Or sit on a doormat and sledge home over the snow on it, you exasperating rodent?

RAT: Do – you – mean – to say, that this doormat doesn't *tell* you anything?

MOLE: Really, Rat. Whoever heard of a doormat *telling* anyone anything?

RAT: Now look here, you – you thick-headed beast, this must stop. Not another word, but scrape – scrape and scratch and dig and hunt round, especially on the sides of the hummocks, if you want to sleep dry and warm tonight, for it's our last chance!

(*Rat digs with absolute fury as Mole scrapes.*)

RAT: Mole! Mole!

MOLE: What is it?

RAT: Come and help, quickly! I've found something.

(*Rat and Mole dig at the same patch.*)

RAT: Hooray-oo-ray-oo-ray-oo-ray!

(*Rat and Mole stand back, observing a solid-looking little door.*)

MOLE: Rat! You're a wonder! A real wonder, that's what you are. You argued it all out, step by step, in that wise head of yours, from the moment that I fell and cut my shin, and you looked at the cut, and at once your majestic mind said to itself, 'Doorscraper!' And then you turned to and found the very doorscraper that done it! Did you stop there? No. Your intellect was working. And of course you found a doormat. 'Now', says you, 'that door exists, as plain as if I saw it. There's nothing else remains to be done but find it!' If only I had your head, Ratty –

RAT: But as you haven't, I suppose you're going to sit on the snow all night and talk? Get up at once and hang onto that bellpull you see there, and ring hard, as hard as you can, while I hammer!

(*Mole starts to ring the bell as Rat hammers on the door.*)

Chapter 3, 'The Wild Wood'

A Monster Called Hex

Hannah Kennedy

Hex is a monster who lives in Taylor's wardrobe. After weeks of being kept awake by fear, Taylor finally decides to confront whatever it is that's lurking in the shadows.

(*Hex hides in the shadows.*)

TAYLOR: I know you're there. Come on. Show yourself, then!

(*No reply.*)

TAYLOR: I'm not scared of you, whoever or whatever you are. Come on!

(*Hex inhales and, then, steps into the light.*)

HEX: Uh. Hi?

(*Taylor screams with fear.*)

HEX: I'm sorry. I didn't mean to scare you. It's okay. I'm not going to hurt you.

(*Taylor takes a moment to catch their breath.*)

TAYLOR: You're the thing that's been living in my wardrobe?

HEX: I'm sorry, I honestly didn't think you would notice.

TAYLOR: What do you mean I wouldn't notice? There's something living in my wardrobe, and that something is you!

(*Pause.*)

TAYLOR: What are you?

HEX: Humans tend to just call me 'monster'.

TAYLOR: Monster?

HEX: Yeah.

TAYLOR: You don't look like very monstery.

HEX: Don't I?

TAYLOR: No. Shouldn't you be hairier?

HEX: I don't think so?

TAYLOR: You'd be scarier with more hair.

HEX: You were already scared of me when you saw me.

TAYLOR: Well, that's because you surprised me. I wasn't really scared.

(*Hex steps towards Taylor. Taylor flinches.*)

HEX: Sure. Not scared.

TAYLOR: I'm not! What are you doing in my wardrobe, anyways?

HEX: It's sort of hard to find somewhere warm and dry to stay when you're a monster. People don't really like us being around.

TAYLOR: I wonder why.

HEX: Yeah, well, that's why we try and find places people won't notice us. Wardrobes, cupboards, under the bed... Small, shadowy spots. But I've never been very good at hiding.

TAYLOR: You can say that again.

HEX: Yeah. Well, I suppose I ought to be going then.

TAYLOR: Going?

HEX: You've found me. It's not like you're going to let me stay in your wardrobe.

TAYLOR: I mean, if it were up to me, I'd consider it, but my dad wouldn't even let me have a fish, never mind a monster. Don't you have parents or something?

HEX: I don't think so.

TAYLOR: You're all alone?

HEX: Yeah.

TAYLOR: Oh.

HEX: Like I said, I should really be going. I need to find somewhere new to hide.

(*Hex turns to leave.*)

TAYLOR: Hey, wait.

(*Hex stops.*)

TAYLOR: Maybe my dad doesn't need to know.

HEX: You mean...?

TAYLOR: You can stay.

HEX: Seriously?!

TAYLOR: For a bit!

HEX: You have no idea what this means to me!

TAYLOR: But if my dad gets even a whiff of you being here –

HEX: I have to go, got it!

TAYLOR: And you need to stop making so much noise at night. I need my sleep.

HEX: You won't hear a peep out of me! I promise.

TAYLOR: Okay. Good.

HEX: This is going to be great!

TAYLOR: So, what do I call you?

HEX: Huh?

TAYLOR: I can't very well just call you 'monster'. You've got to have a name?

(*Pause.*)

TAYLOR: You do have a name, right?

HEX: I do... It's just... It's just nobody has ever asked me before.

TAYLOR: Well, I'm asking.

(*Taylor holds out their hand.*)

TAYLOR: Nice to meet you. My name is Taylor. What's your name?

HEX: Hex. My name's Hex.

(*Hex takes Taylor's hand and shakes it.*)

Tuesday
Alison Carr

On what would appear to be an ordinary Tuesday, the sky splits in half over a schoolyard and the pupils are sucked into a parallel dimension. In the new dimension, they meet their parallel selves: the 'Us' and 'Them' collide. Mack (one of 'Us') and Cam (one of 'Them') are from different dimensions. In this scene, they explore the differences between their worlds. The genders and pronouns of these characters can be altered as required.

(*Cam loiters. He's keeping to himself, but Mack sees him.*)

MACK: You. You.

CAM: Me?

MACK: Yes. I don't know you. Are you from up there?

CAM: Yes.

MACK: Why didn't you speak up when they were asking who else fell through?

(*Cam shrugs.*)

MACK: Did you really fall through the ground from another universe?

CAM: 'Spose so.

MACK: What's your name?

CAM: Cam.

MACK: Why don't we have a Cam here?

(*Cam shrugs.*)

MACK: Do you have a me up there?

CAM: Dunno.

MACK: Oh you'd know. Everybody knows me.

(*Cam shrugs.*)

MACK: What's that?

CAM: An orange.

MACK: A what?

CAM: An orange.

MACK: What's that?

CAM: You don't have oranges?

MACK: No.

CAM: It's like, a fruit.

MACK: A what?

CAM: You don't have fruit?

MACK: No.

CAM: It's good for you.

MACK: What does an orange taste like?

CAM: Like... sort of like... it tastes like... an orange.

MACK: Like chicken?

CAM: No.

MACK: Like liquorice?

CAM: No.

MACK: Like cabbage?

CAM: No.

MACK: That's a shame.

CAM: Sorry.

MACK: I'm only joking with you, stupid. I know what an orange is. Why are you holding it?

CAM: It's all I've got from up there.

MACK: It'll get sorted out, they'll find a way to get you back.

CAM: I don't know if I want to go back.

MACK: Why not?

CAM: Here might be better.

MACK: Why do you say that?

CAM: You know when you just want the ground to open and swallow you up?

MACK: Yeah.

CAM: It did. And it was great.

MACK: What were you doing when it happened?

CAM: Eating my lunch behind the new Science block.

MACK: What new Science block?

CAM: Our school has a new Science block.

MACK: Ours doesn't. Mind you, I hate Science. Why were you eating your lunch there?

CAM: It's quiet. And they leave me alone.

MACK: They?

CAM: I'd been off school for ages with glandular fever. Today was my first day back. Mr Simmons pointed me out in registration, said 'welcome back' and made everyone turn around and say it too. He's horrible, Mr Simmons. I hate him. Do you have him here?

MACK: Yeah.

CAM: What's he like?

MACK: Horrible.

CAM: So everyone said 'welcome back' and I said 'thank you' and smiled. Tried to. Sometimes in photos I think I'm smiling then when I see it I look like I'm having a really difficult poo.

(*Beat.*)

MACK: I look great in photos.

Pigeon English

Gbolahan Obisesan, adapted from the novel by **Stephen Kelman**

Having arrived in London from Ghana, Harri lives with his sister Lydia and their Mum on the ninth floor of a block of flats in a London housing estate. In an unfamiliar environment, Harri must navigate fights, family and murder. In this scene, Harri tries to cheer Lydia up on her birthday.

HARRI: I had to make Lydia laugh. If I didn't make her laugh the whole day would be finished.

Come on, sweetheart – Chin up –

(*No response from Lydia.*)

HARRI: Nothing – Not even a tiny smile.

(*No response from Lydia.*)

HARRI: Turn your frown upside down – You know it makes sense.

(*No response from Lydia.*)

HARRI: Nothing again.

(*No response from Lydia.*)

HARRI: You are my sunshine, my only sunshine.

LYDIA: Stop it – (*Suppressing a smile.*)

HARRI: Rub a dub dub, no need to blub – I love you from the heart of my bottom.

LYDIA: Stop it – (*Smiling.*)

HARRI: Got you – I win –

(*Lydia laughs out loud.*)

HARRI: Do you want my presents? You have to follow me, it's outside.

LYDIA: Gowayou – I'm not falling for another trick.

HARRI: It's not a trick, I promise –
Just come on, scaredy cat –

LYDIA: Where are we going?

HARRI: You'll see – Just trust me –

(*Harri and Lydia leave. Lydia searches unsuccessfully for her present. Harri looks on with excitement.*)

HARRI: (*To audience.*) It felt brutal.

LYDIA: Just give me my present and let's go – Where is it?

HARRI: Right in front of you – The cement was still wet. The council man was gone for his chop. If you were going to do it, it had to be now. You couldn't plan it any better.

LYDIA: What am I supposed to be doing here?

HARRI: Just jump – It'll be brutal – Your footprints will get struck and when it dries they'll be trapped forever – Then the ramp and the whole tower will belong to us. You have to jump quite hard though. You have to mean it.

LYDIA: That's stupid – I'm not jumping in that –

HARRI: Go on – It will only take one second – You put your footprints in it and I'll write your name next to them so everybody knows. We'll both do it. I'll go first.

(*Harri positions himself, before jumping with both feet into the cement. Harri squats pushing the weight of his body down to make better indentation in the cement.*)

LYDIA: It looks like you're doing a poo –

HARRI: It's the best way – Just watch me – 1, 2, 3, 4, 5, 6, 7, 8, 9 10

(*Harri does a little twist and jumps back out of the cement.*)

HARRI: Look you can see the Diadora signs under my trainers –

LYDIA: You're so lame –

HARRI: Just do it, lazy face – You can't give a present back if somebody plans it for you. It's like saying you hate them.

LYDIA: Ok – Ok –

(*Lydia jumps next to Harri's footprint. She squats into a similar position as Harri. Her lips move quietly as she counts to ten.*)

HARRI: Now give it a little twist –

LYDIA: I'm twisting – I'm twisting –

(*Lydia struggles to jump back out. Her feet are stuck and unbalanced, she nearly falls. Lydia screams.*)

LYDIA: Help me – Help me –

HARRI: Don't panic, I've got you –

(*Harri pulls Lydia out of the cement.*)

LYDIA: Quick and write the names before it goes too dry –

(*Harri drops down to write both their names under the footprints.*)

HARRI: Asweh, it looked bo-styles.

(*Lydia is smiling in delirious delight.*)

HARRI: Happy birthday – I told you you'd love it.

Scene 27, 'Lydia's Birthday'

Coram Boy

Helen Edmundson, adapted from the novel by **Jamila Gavin**

Growing up in the 1750s, two boys – TOBY (black), and Aaron (white) – are best friends. They met when living at the Coram orphanage. Yet when Aaron is apprenticed as a musician, Toby is sent to live with a slave trader called Mr Gaddarn. At the beginning of this scene, Aaron is singing in the drawing room at Mr Gaddarn's house, where Toby is serving delicacies from a silver tray.

AARON: Tobes! You look splendid. And look at this place. It's like a palace!

TOBY: Why haven't you been to visit me?

AARON: Sorry. We've been rehearsing for the concert all the time. And when they said we were coming here, I thought it would be a good surprise for you.

TOBY: I don't like surprises any more.

(*He walks away.*)

AARON: Toby?

TOBY: I'm not allowed to speak to people.

(*In a quiet corner of the room, Aaron catches up with Toby.*)

AARON: Don't walk off. What's wrong?

TOBY: As if you care.

AARON: I'm sorry I didn't come before. You could have come and seen me, you know.

TOBY: I'm not allowed out.

AARON: Look.

(*He takes the bag of toffees out of his pocket and offers them to Toby.*)

Mr Ledbury gave me them. I saved half for you.

TOBY: (*Taking them.*) Thanks.

(*He turns away and starts to cry.*)

AARON: Tobes? Are you crying?

TOBY: No.

AARON: What's wrong? Aren't you happy here? Tobes?

TOBY: I hate it.

AARON: But why? It's amazing.

TOBY: You don't know what it's like.

AARON: Look... why don't we go to your room and you can tell...

TOBY: I haven't got a room.

AARON: Where do you sleep? (*Toby doesn't reply.*) Toby.

TOBY: Can we go and find my mother?

AARON: What?

TOBY: I want to go soon. Tomorrow or the day after.

AARON: Tobes, I can't. We're going to all these big houses to sing. And it's the concert in a few weeks. And I like it at Mr Brook's. He's kind and he never shouts and I love the music.

TOBY: Just go away.

AARON: If you're not happy you should tell Mr Gaddarn.

TOBY: He's horrible. He's going to cut my tongue out.

AARON: Cut your tongue out? Don't be silly.

TOBY: You don't believe me!

AARON: I...

TOBY: I'm going to find my mother. Soon! And you're not coming. She's my mother anyway!

(*He walks out of the room. Sadly, Aaron goes back to join the other Coram Boys. Toby enters a dark room. It is wood-panelled, with long leaded windows that look out over the docks. There is the shadowy outline of maps on the walls, and books on high shelves. He crosses to a large globe which stands in the corner of the room. He squats down next to it and turns it until he finds Africa.*)

TOBY: Africa.

(*With his finger, he traces a line.*)

London. The Indies.

(*He takes his mother's beads out of his pocket and rubs them between his fingers.*)

I'm coming soon. I'm coming soon.

(*He curls up on the floor next to the map and sobs.*)

Act 2, Scenes 9-10

Sherbet
Sarah McDonald-Hughes and **Curtis Cole**

Set in the yard of Jade and Nathan's mum's house, Moss Side, August 1997. Ten-year-old Jade stands in the middle of the yard. Six-year-old Nathan has his back to the back wall of the yard. They are playing Bulldog, a tag-based game where one player attempts to intercept the other players as they run from one side of the designated area to the other.

JADE: Chicken.

NATHAN: Not.

JADE: Baby. Scaredy cat. Wuss.

NATHAN: Shut up!

JADE: Run then.

NATHAN: Don't want to.

JADE: Cos you're a lickle baby.

NATHAN: I'm not!

(*Beat.*)

Why can't I be on?

JADE: Because I'm on. Run!

NATHAN: It's not fair. You're supposed to take turns.

JADE: (*Changing tack.*) I'll give you... two second head start.

(*Nathan considers this.*)

NATHAN: Need a drink.

JADE: Chicken.

NATHAN: I'm gonna get a drink.

(*He moves to go; she grabs him.*)

JADE: Ha! You're on.

NATHAN: I weren't playing then.

JADE: Tough, you're on now.

NATHAN: I don't want to be on. I don't even like Bulldog. Stupid. Getting a drink.

(*Jade jumps, huge and over the top.*)

JADE: Oh my god there's a rat –

(*Nathan jumps, terrified.*)

NATHAN: Where?

JADE: There.

(*She points. They both watch. Nothing.*)

NATHAN: Nah.

JADE: Swear down.

NATHAN: Liar.

(*They watch. Something moves. They both jump.*)

JADE: Am I a liar?

NATHAN: Get it away!

JADE: Am I liar though?

NATHAN: Alright (you're not)!

(*He watches the rat.*)

NATHAN: It's horrible.

JADE: What you crying for?

NATHAN: I'm not crying.

JADE: Nothing to be scared of.

NATHAN: I'm not scared.

JADE: Only a little rat.

NATHAN: Disgusting.

JADE: You're disgusting. What's wrong with you? Scared it's going to get you?

NATHAN: It's horrible. You're horrible.

JADE: You're horrible.

(*He tries the door. It's locked. He can't work it out; rattles it.*)

JADE: Give it here –

(*She shoves him out of the way and tries to open it.*)

JADE: Why's it locked?

NATHAN: Are we in trouble?

JADE: No. It's fine. He probably just wants mum to rest properly without kids and noise. She's nearly better, you know.

NATHAN: For real?

JADE: Yeah. Neil said soon she'll be totally normal and we can go out and stuff.

NATHAN: And she won't stay in bed no more?

JADE: Mmm.

(*Nathan jumps.*)

NATHAN: Get it away from me!

(*Jade listens at the door. Nathan screams.*)

NATHAN: Jade help! It's after me!

JADE: Sssh, I'm trying to listen. Something's happening.

(*Nathan finds a brick on the floor. He throws it at the rat, hitting it.*)

NATHAN: Got it!

(*He goes over to the dead rat. He picks up the brick and hits the rat a few more times. Jade doesn't clock, keeps listening at the door.*)

NATHAN: Yeah. Die, rat! Look, Jade! I got it!

JADE: Mum's up.

(*Beat.*)

NATHAN: Is she? Is she better now?

JADE: No, I don't know.

(*Nathan goes to the door and shakes it.*)

JADE: Don't do that –

NATHAN: It's not fair. Zack's inside!

JADE: He's a baby, int he? And he's asleep, he won't cause no mither.

NATHAN: I won't cause mither! I've been helping! I gave Zack his medicine and stopped him crying, didn't I?

JADE: Yeah, only cos I told you to.

NATHAN: I want Mum.

(*Nathan goes to the door and shouts.*)

NATHAN: Mum? Are you alright?

JADE: Ssssh! If you wake Zack up again Neil'll kill you.

(*Nathan looks scared.*)

JADE: Come on, come here.

(*Jade goes to him, leads him away from the door, almost kind.*)

JADE: Bulldog. You're on.

Scene 1

Hamlet

William Shakespeare, adapted by LAMDA

Hamlet, Prince of Denmark, is revenging his father's death, who died at the hand of his Uncle Claudius. Feigning madness, Hamlet is sent away to England. As Hamlet is returning to Denmark, he stumbles across a Gravedigger.

HAMLET: Whose grave's this, sirrah?

GRAVEDIGGER: Mine, sir.

(*Sings.*) O, a pit of clay for to be made –

HAMLET: I think it be thine indeed, for thou liest in't.

GRAVEDIGGER: You lie out on't, sir, and therefore 'tis not yours. For my part, I do not lie in't, yet it is mine.

HAMLET: Thou dost lie in't, to be in't and say 'tis thine. 'Tis for the dead, not for the quick: therefore thou liest.

GRAVEDIGGER: 'Tis a quick lie, sir; 'twill away again from me to you.

HAMLET: What man dost thou dig it for?

GRAVEDIGGER: For no man, sir.

HAMLET: What woman then?

GRAVEDIGGER: For none neither.

HAMLET: Who is to be buried in't?

GRAVEDIGGER: One that was a woman, sir; but rest her soul, she's dead.

HAMLET: (*Aside.*) How absolute the knave is.

How long hast thou been a grave-maker?

GRAVEDIGGER: Of all the days i'th' year I came to't that day that our last King Hamlet o'ercame Fortinbras.

HAMLET: How long is that since?

GRAVEDIGGER: Cannot you tell that? Every fool can tell that. It was the very day that young Hamlet was born – he that is mad and sent into England.

HAMLET: Ay, marry. Why was he sent into England?

GRAVEDIGGER: Why, because a was mad. A shall recover his wits there. Or if a do not, 'tis no great matter there.

HAMLET: Why?

GRAVEDIGGER: 'Twill not be seen in him there. There the men are as mad as he.

HAMLET: How came he mad?

GRAVEDIGGER: Very strangely, they say.

HAMLET: How 'strangely'?

GRAVEDIGGER: Faith, e'en with losing his wits.

HAMLET: Upon what ground?

GRAVEDIGGER: Why, here in Denmark.

HAMLET: How long will a man lie i'th' earth ere he rot?

GRAVEDIGGER: Faith, if a be not rotten before a die – as we have many pocky corses nowadays that will scarce hold the laying in – a will last you some eight year or nine year. A tanner will last you nine year.

HAMLET: Why he more than another?

GRAVEDIGGER: Why, sir, his hide is so tanned with his trade that a will keep out water a great while, and your water is a sore decayer of your whoreson dead body. Here's a skull now hath lien you i'th' earth three and twenty years.

HAMLET: Whose was it?

GRAVEDIGGER: A whoreson mad fellow's it was. Whose do you think it was?

HAMLET: Nay, I know not.

GRAVEDIGGER: A pestilence on him for a mad rogue! A poured a flagon of Rhenish on my head once. This same skull, sir, was Yorick's skull, the King's jester.

HAMLET: This? (*Takes the skull.*)

GRAVEDIGGER: E'en that.

HAMLET: Alas, poor Yorick!

Act 5, Scene 1

The Sweetness of a Sting

Chinonyerem Odimba

When Badger's parents decide they want to return to their home country, fifteen-year-old Badger is forced to confront the idea that he might have to leave his life behind. Running away, Badger enters a dream-world of talking ants, ladybirds and spiders. In this scene, Badger comes across an Army of Ants.

(The Army Ants enter, fifteen in number – in single file, movements precise and synchronised. They are military like and orderly, and all their movements should be such. They halt in front of Badger. One Ant steps out of line.)

ANT: At ease!

(Beat.)

(Ant steps forward.)

ANT: At ease!

BADGER: Are you talking to me?

ANT: Obey.

Obey.

BADGER: –

ANT: Crimes against the Queen number one – will not obey. We will have to force him to do it our way.

BADGER: What are you saying?

(Ant walks and stands face to face to Badger.)

ANT: *(Barks.)* Crimes against the Queen number two – will not listen.

BADGER: Listen?

You need to back off –

ANT: Back off?

BADGER: Yeah step away before...
You don't know me!
What you think you can just threaten me? Badger –

ANT: Badger, Badger, Badger...
Do you know who we are?

BADGER: Ants, by the looks of things!

(*Ant repositions, brandishing their stick as a weapon.*)

ANT: Crimes against the Queen number three – trespasser.
We demand a direct answer...

Do as we say or take your last breath...
We will inflict a very painful death –

BADGER: How exactly are you going to do that?

ANT: Look how many of us there are.
Your talking back is bizarre.

Why did you not come with your own army?
What kind of fool takes such a journey?

Surrender or obey.
This is the only way.

Strange looking boy, you will not win.
We will wipe off that grin...

(*Ant lifts their stick above their head, threatening.*)

BADGER: Yeah, got that!

ANT: Stranger to threaten our Queen.

BADGER: What Queen?

ANT: Our Queen,
Our beautiful Queen.
The giver of life.
It is in her name we strive,
To remember what has been.
There is no greater allegiance than our allegiance to the Queen.
For her every morning we say a prayer –
She is our most valuable player.

BADGER: That's cool. I was just hoping you could just show me the way out of whatever this is. The spiders –

ANT: The spiders were here?

BADGER: Yeah, but they're gone now, and I really need to go home.

ANT: You can't go anywhere.
Once you are here it is very rare...
To escape,
This landscape.

Did the spiders not tell you that?

BADGER: You know what – I'm gone!

(*Ant tries to stop him leaving.*)

ANT: This camp is surrounded by the hive wall –

BADGER: Just move out of my way –

ANT: No one can go through it except the Queen.

BADGER: Where's the Queen then?

She brought me here she can take me back.

(*Ant laughs.*)

ANT: If you want to leave here you must surrender.
We need to be sure that you won't offend her.
You see this is the way it is...
The story we have to tell of what caused this
Is why you are here we guess
But we can't tell it unless...

BADGER: Fine. I give in!

I surrender.

Now can you please tell me what I need to know to get out of here.

Scene 3

Wolfie

Ross Willis

A and Z are twins and unborn babies. On the hottest day of the year, the twins are about to be born. This scene explores their relationship and excitement for the world outside the womb.

(*Just a typical day for the Twins floating and chilling in the womb.*)

A: We da Twins.

Z: We da Sharky Twins.

A: gonna be born ten weeks too early!

Z: Wait what? –

A: We da Twins –

Z: We haven't discussed this.

A: I've made an executive decision.

Z: I'm not fully cooked yet.

A: get your game face on yo.

Z: But it's cosy in here!

A: Five.
Four.

Z: My head isn't squishy enough!

A: THREE!!

Z: It's not time in da story!

A: Movin da story on!

Z: WAIT!

A: What!?

Z: Scared.

A: No.

Z: Don't.

A: Am.
I'll be wiv you.

Z: Don't let go.

A: Right now da old-ass sun is off her face on heat.

Z: Right now dere is a Hungry Woman in a shop.

A: Our mum.

Z: Da Hungry Woman is countin pennies.
One penny.
Two penny.

A: Three penny. Four penny.
Slams down a packet of Cup-a-Soup.

Z: Chicken flavour.

A: good choice.
Hungry
Hands fumblin Woman lookin needs ninety to da floor. pennies.
Self-service machine judgin her.
unexpected poverty in da baggin area.

Z: Hungry Woman ain't got ninety pennies. She ain't even close yo.
Kick.

A: Kick.
Men wiv hands full of pennies tuttin behind her.
Tut.

Z: Tut.
Suddenly dere is a gush.

A: A tsunami breakin from her.

Z: Pourin out of her.

A: Floodin da store.

Z: Drops da Cup-a-Soup.

A: Swept away by da waves.

Z: Sobbin covers up her rumblin stomach.

A: Poor Mummy Sharky.
Kick.

Z: Kick.

A: Layin on a hospital bed screamin on da hottest day of da year wasn't da plan.

Z: Her contractions contradict her.

A: Ice-cream truck jingle tryin to harmonise to her screams.

Z: STOP.

A: MOVE!

Z: CAN'T!

A: See you on da other side loser.

(*A puts on a crash helmet and goggles and begins to be born.*)

Ultimate road trip.
Cruisin down dat highway.
Car

Wind top in open. my hair.
Super slumber party over.
Twist and turn! Twist and turn!
Squeeze! Squeeze! Squeeze!

Z: Inhumane HOOOOOWLS!
Hungry Woman feelin like her spine is gonna snap snap snap away!

A: Floatin on a cloud of rainbows!

Z: Feelin like she's bein ripped ripped ripped apart by fire!

A: Floatin on a cloud of rainbows!
Twist and turn! Twist and turn!
Squeeze! Squeeze! Squeeze!

(*A is born. Sees the world for the first time. It's an overwhelming sensory experience for A.*)

A: WOAAAAAAAAAH!
You gotta come out here yo!

Z: No!

A: DIS IS AMAZIN!
Yo, come on out or I'm draggin you out myself.
Hungry Woman has her eyes shut shut shut.
Hair like Cheesestrings coverin her face.

Z: Da Super Woman starts round two.

A: DINg! DINg!

Z: Sun knockin on da window tryin to get in.
Baby knockin on da door tryin to get out.

A: Da Super Woman is pushin.
Fightin against da pain in her body.
Fightin like she's had to fight her entire life.

She'll never get credit for dis moment.
Dis amazin moment.
Dis amazin Super Woman.
I see her and she is so beautiful.
She makes my heart sparkle and breathe glitter for her.
Like an inner light of love so bright that the old-ass sun thinks we're comin for its job.

(*A sparkles and breathes glitter mum.*)

(*Z is born. It's much less graceful. Actually frankly it's pretty messy. Z then sparkles and breathes glitter mum. Z mouths 'wow'.*)

Z: Dis feels amazin.

The First Chapter, Scene 1

Level 1 Acting: Grade 3 Solo

A-Typical Rainbow

JJ Green

Boy, who has Autism Spectrum Disorder (ASD), is at school. In class, he observes his teacher's mannerisms and presentation. Boy realises that his teacher is struggling and asks if she is okay.

BOY: She said she was fine but everything around her added up to something else. I may not be able to do long division without getting distracted but surely everyone can see that?

Can't they?

Ten a.m. she enters the classroom and slightly trips on the rug. That rug has always been there. It's *her* rug.

Ten-oh-four she missed Georgia off the register.

Ten thirty-two she started the class two minutes, exactly a hundred and twenty seconds late. She was never late. Ten forty-one spelled 'Morning' M-O-U-R-N-I-N-G on the whiteboard. Ten fifty-seven checks her phone under the desk, you can tell because the light slightly illuminated her glasses enough to see a brief moment of reflection as the Nokia screen danced across her lenses. Eleven twenty-eight a.m. dismisses us exactly a hundred and twenty seconds early for breaktime, remains behind in the classroom despite it being chocolate biscuit day. Those are her favourite. She said those were her favourite. You remember people's favourite things. That and carrot cake which is gross. She has no taste. We return from playtime. Murder scene. Exhibit A: coffee cup still on desk exactly where she left it approximately seventy degrees from her untouched pile of papers. Coffee mug empty, kettle remains by the sink untouched. Exhibit B: whiteboard hasn't been rubbed down from last lesson. It's always rubbed down from the last lesson to hide her spelling mistakes. Exhibit C: new addition to attire: small scrunched-up tissue being held to wrist by watch strap. Watch is on time. D: slightly messy hair on the right side of her head indicating a phone has been held. E: phone charger attached to rear desk plug. F: nail on left-hand index finger where immaculate polish once stood is now chipped, bitten. G: ever so slight red mark on right side of face, she's been leaning on it. H: pigeon hole remains empty no papers collected from staff room.

Clearly this is a woman who's falling apart at the seams.

Miss, are you okay?

Scene 5, 'Parent's Evening/Murder in a Classroom'

Little Women

Anne-Marie Casey, adapted from the novel by **Louisa May Alcott**

Beth is the second youngest of the March sisters. She is very unwell with scarlet fever. In this speech, Beth speaks to her older sister Jo. Beth acknowledges the reality of her death, expresses how much she'll miss her family, and encourages Jo to embrace her own life.

(*Beth, who is indeed very fragile looking, is lying on the sofa. Beth reaches her hand across to Jo, who starts to cry.*)

BETH: Jo dear, I'm glad you know it. I've tried to tell Pa and Marmee and Meg, but I couldn't. I'm not getting better. I'm getting worse. I've known it for a good while and now I'm used to it, though sometimes it's still hard to bear.

I want to get better. I try but every day I lose a little bit of strength, I feel more tired. It's like the tide, it goes slowly but it can't be stopped.

Jo, I'm grown up now and I have to believe this is what God wants for me or I can't. You must speak to Pa and Marmee. The doctor says that the people who love you the most are the blindest to such things. I asked the doctor to tell me the truth and although I'm sure it cost him dearly he did. He told me it was hopeless, Jo, but that I would not suffer too much at the end. I was so scared of that you see.

I don't know how to express myself, and shouldn't try to anyone but you because I can't speak expect to you. I only mean to say, that I have a feeling that it was never intended I should live long. I'm not like the rest of you; I never made any plans; I never thought of being married, I couldn't seem to imagine myself anything but stupid little Beth trotting about at home, of no use anywhere but there. I never wanted to go away, and the hard part now is the leaving you all. I try not to be afraid, but it seems as if I should be homesick for you even in heaven. (*Pause.*) Don't hope any more, Jo; it won't do any good, I'm sure of that. We won't be miserable, but enjoy this time together. You have to promise to help me, Jo. Then when I'm gone, you have to help Pa and Marmee as Meg will have John and the new baby to comfort her and Amy will have her new, wonderful life.

I'm not so good as everyone thinks, but I have tried to do right and I know that you and I have loved each other as much as any two sisters could. You must keep writing your splendid books when it's hard remember that.

Act 2, Scene 14, 'The March House'

Life of Pi

Lolita Chakrabarti, adapted from the novel by **Yann Martel**

Pi is an Indian boy in his teenage years. Pi is stranded in a lifeboat in the Pacific Ocean with Richard Parker, a Royal Bengal tiger. So far, Pi has encountered zebras and hyenas, sea turtles and orangutans. At the start of this speech, Pi and Richard Parker have been without water for ten days. They stumble across an enchanting island, but it is much more ominous than they first think.

(*Pi puts a hand out of the boat and feels solid ground.*)

PI: Land! Firm, solid, rooted land! Allah be praised!

(*He stands up.*)

I crawl to a glittering lake of cool, fresh water. I drink and drink and suddenly I can see again! It's an island! It's so green and lush. We're in paradise. 'Hello?! Hello? Is anyone there?' A babble of voices answer me.

(*A cacophony of chattering meerkats reply.*)

Meerkats, thousands of them. I have company!

(*Richard Parker exits.*)

Richard Parker runs inland but I'm so drowsy I'm falling asleep in the boat. I watch all the meerkats climb up to sleep in the trees. I was so happy I could've stayed there forever. A few nights later, I saw something bobbing in the lake, it looked like a dead shark. It dissolved in the water and I thought I must've dreamt it. And then wonder of wonders I found fruit – fragrant, juicy, ripe fruit, at the top of a tall tree. I clambered up, plucked that fruit and took an enormous bite. It was the best thing I'd ever tasted, dripping down my chin, sticky and sweet, but there was something hard inside it and when I took it out of my mouth, I saw it was a human tooth. I tore open another fruit, there was a molar in it and then another, it was the same. It was almost dark, the air was thick with scent, I was getting drowsy again but I knew I had to get to the boat. I ran. The ground burned my feet and that's when I understood – that island was carnivorous. It lured me in with fresh water by the day then deadened my senses at night turning to acid, digesting any flesh it could find. That was a shark I'd seen in the water. That's why the meerkats slept in the trees! They were trying to warn me.

(*Frantic squealing of meerkats.*)

I had to leave, I ran for the boat but I could hear Richard Parker howling in pain.

(*Richard Parker howls.*)

I couldn't leave him. He'd saved my life.

Scene 11, 'At Sea' – Scene 12, 'The Hospital Room'

A Little Princess

Frances Hodgson Burnett, adapted by LAMDA

Sara is enrolled in boarding school by her father who serves in the Army. Upon her father's death, eleven-year-old Sara is left an orphan with nowhere to go. The stern headmistress Miss Minchin takes away all of Sara's possessions and forces her to live in a cold, worn attic, away from all her friends. At the start of this speech, Lottie discovers Sara's living situation.

SARA: Lottie! How did you get in here? No – shh. Shh. You must be quiet. Miss Minchin will be very angry with me if she finds you here. You mustn't cry or make any noise. Okay?

(Lottie is looking around the room, shocked. Sara follows her gaze.)

It's – it's not such a bad room, Lottie. Look – you can see all sorts of things you can't see downstairs. Like chimneys – quite close to us – with smoke curling up in wreaths and clouds and going up into the sky – and sparrows hopping around and talking to each other just as if they were people – and other attic windows where heads may pop out any minute and you can wonder who they belong to. And it all feels as high up as if it was another world.

(Sara peers out of the attic window.)

Come here and you can see. I wish someone lived over there! It is so close that if there was somebody in the attic, we could talk to each other through the windows and climb over to see each other, if we were not afraid of falling. And look at that sparrow!

(Sara giggles and walks around the room.)

We're so high above everything it's almost like a nest in a tree. The slanting ceiling is so funny. See, you can scarcely stand up at this end of the room; and when the morning begins to come, I can lie in bed and look right into the sky through that flat window in the roof. It is like a square patch of light. If the sun is going to shine, little pink clouds float about, and I feel as if I could touch them. And if it rains, the drops patter and patter as if they were saying something nice. Then if there are stars, you can lie and try to count how many go into the patch. It takes such a lot. And just look at that tiny, rusty grate in the corner. If it was polished and there was a fire in it, just think how nice it would be. You see, it's really a beautiful little room.

(*Sara hears noises downstairs.*)

You must go, Lottie – before Miss Minchin finds you here. Quick. And remember to be quiet!

(*Sara ushers Lottie downstairs and re-enters her attic, alone. She stands in the middle and looks around. She sits down and lets her head drop in her hands.*)

It's a lonely place. Sometimes it's the loneliest place in the world.

Chapter 9

Blue Tongue

Evan Placey

Jamie is at the GP's, chatting to the doctor about their fluorescent blue tongue.
They try to convince the doctor to agree to their plan before their Mum re-enters
the room.

JAMIE: Let's level with each other, yeah?

Human to human.

Let's pretend you're not in the doctor coat, and I'm not in the school uniform
blazer.

We're just two people who have about two minutes to come to an agreement
before my mother comes back in here.

And we know how this is going to go down.

You're going to reassure her there's nothing wrong –

She's going to insist there clearly is – it's not every day her child has a
fluorescent blue tongue –

And she'll start threatening all kinds of things – local press, a lawsuit, maybe
even our street WhatsApp group, since most of them are your patients too and
that group is vicious –

I mean you don't want to have been there when someone put out their bins on
the wrong day and a fox decorated the pavement with all manner of colourful
debris – chicken bones and fish and chips grease-paper and some Play-Doh or
perhaps moldy birthday cake icing, hard to tell – let's just say Joseph and the
Technicolor Dreamcoat has nothing on the gaudy patchwork of stuff scattered
about our street that day.

And so just as mum's yelling about second opinions and how everyone on our
street is going to leave your surgery, you'll be tempted to calmly explain my blue
tongue is merely a byproduct of having stolen a blue lolly from the box mum
bought for my little sister's birthday party bags next week.

Now. I would argue that 'stolen' is a pretty strong word given they were sitting
on the table, packet open, taunting me.

But the fact remains that Mum would turn her ire away from you and onto
me and it's unlikely then that the videogame I asked for will be making an
appearance anytime soon.

So.

Good Doctor. What I'm asking is that you simply tell my mum – in fifty-seven
seconds when she returns – that I do in fact have some kind of terrible illness.
While you are very clever – you went to med school afterall – or so I'm assuming
or you've got bigger problems than me – even the smartest person would

struggle to come up with something in the next forty-four seconds. Not to fear, doc, for I have come armed with my own diagnosis.

The giraffe.

Because I bet you didn't know that giraffes have blue tongues.

But I, the saviour of your career and the street WhatsApp group, do know this.

And it just conveniently happens that my class made a trip to the Zoo just last week.

Sometimes fate does have a way of helping out. So you just need to tell Mum that the blue-tongued giraffe transmitted some of its saliva when I was feeding it.

Or maybe it's some sort of airborne –

Or like birdflu

Or madcow

Or

Look I can't do everything for you doc, you need to take a bit of initiative.

I have every faith in you.

And look, there's a delicious blue lollipop in it for you if you pull this off.

Okay, here we go – I'd know the squeak of those shoes anywhere.

And as ironic as it feels saying this to my doctor:

Break a leg, Doc.

Dido, Queen of Carthage

Christopher Marlowe, adapted by LAMDA

Following a storm at sea, Trojan soldier Aeneas finds refuge in Carthage, which is ruled by Queen Dido. Although Aeneas thinks himself safe, the Gods decide to interfere. Goddess Venus sends Cupid – disguised as Aeneas' son (Ascanius) – to prick Dido with his arrow, forcing her to fall madly in love with Aeneas. Dido and Aeneas' all-consuming relationship begins. However, fate dictates that Aeneas must build a new Troy in Italy. In this speech, Hermes – the Messenger God – arrives with the real Ascanius and urges Aeneas to attend to his fate in Italy.

(*Enter Hermes with Ascanius.*)

HERMES: Aeneas, stay! Jove's herald bids thee stay.
Why, cousin, stand you building cities here,
And beautifying the empire of this queen,
While Italy is clean out of thy mind?
Too, too forgetful of thine own affairs,
Why wilt thou so betray thy son's good hap?
The king of gods sent me from highest heav'n,
To sound this angry message in thine ears:
Vain man, what monarchy expect'st thou here?
Or with what thought sleep'st thou on Lybia's shore?
If that all glory hath forsaken thee,
And thou despise the praise of such attempts;
Yet think upon Ascanius' prophecy,
And young Iulus, more than thousand years,
Whom I have brought from Ida, where he slept,
And bore young Cupid unto Cypress Isle.

(*Aeneas tries to speak to Ascanius.*)

Spend'st thou thy time about this little boy,
And giv'st not ear unto the charge I bring?
I tell thee, thou must straight to Italy,
Or else abide the wrath of frowning Jove.

(*Hermes exits.*)

Act 5, Scene 1

Proud

Hannah Kennedy

Frankie is getting ready for their school prom. Their mother is disappointed that they have decided not to wear the outfit picked out for them.

FRANKIE: Before you say anything, I know! I know this isn't what you picked out for me. I know that this isn't how you wanted me to wear my hair, either. I know nothing about the way that I look right now is what you had in mind, but here's the thing, mum, I don't want to look like what you have in mind.

I tried it on, what you picked out, I did, and I tried so, so hard to like it. I wanted to like it for you but I can't. Because it doesn't look like me. That shade of green isn't me. The way it fits around my neck and my hips doesn't feel like me. I stood in front of the mirror, and I stared at myself, I took in every single inch of me from the tips of my toes all the way to the top of my head, and it felt like I was looking at a different person. As if the very atoms of who I am had transformed me into a person that I didn't recognise.

And this is my day. This is my prom. And I've spent my entire life trying to be the person that you want me to be. Be your Frankie. And I've wanted to want that for so long. Every morning, I would wake up and wish that I would want to be the person that you see, but I'm not. I have never been that person, and trying to be that person is rotting me from the inside out.

And I think you know that, don't you? You can see that I hate myself. Actually, no, that's not true. I don't hate myself. I hate the version of me that you think I am, that you think I should be. I love the real me. I love the person I am when I'm with my friends, I love the sound of my name when my friends say it, I love the way I hold myself, I love the way I laugh. I love all the parts of myself that I am too terrified to let you see in case I disappoint you.

But I think I've realised now that I'll always disappoint you. So, I might as well be me with my full chest because spending my prom being miserable is not worth it for a few photos that you'd like to stick in the family album.

This is what I'm wearing to prom. And I like the way I look in it, I like the way I feel in it.

And I hope you'll find it in your heart to be proud of me anyway.

Crusaders

Frances Poet

Across the globe, children and teenagers make their way to the 'Holy Land' following visions that the world will end. Seventeen-year-old Meera makes her way to Mount Hermon from Scotland. Halfway up the mountain, her friend Kayleigh dies. In this speech, Meera tries to contact her mum.

(Mount Hermon. Night. Meera is alone. She is wearing many layers of clothes but she is still shivering. It is freezing. She looks at the battery level on her phone and considers. She puts it back in her pocket then, on impulse, changes her mind, pulls it out and dials.)

MEERA: Mum, it's me. I –

(It's her mum's answer machine. She is winded by the disappointment of it. She waits for the beep.)

Hi. You're working the night shift. I pictured you sitting by the phone waiting for my call but I suppose... life goes on. It's me by the way. Meera. Sorry I didn't answer your calls. Maybe you've given up? I'm on a new phone so I don't know if you've been trying me... My old one got a bit... wet. I can't speak for long because I'm low on battery and this is my only torch so... It's so dark here. And cold. I told Kayleigh. I told her it would be freezing at night but she was determined to ditch her layers. It was so hot and the climb was...

I'm on a mountain called Mount Hermon. It's probably where Jesus was transfigured into divine form. It might also have been where Moses was given the Ten Commandments. Lots of people have different theories why we might come here as opposed to, I don't know, Mecca or Machu Picchu or Kashi Vishwanath or Glastonbury Tor. I wish it had been Glastonbury. You could have driven us.

The Arabs just call it Snow Mountain but Hermon has a really complicated meaning in Hebrew. An Israeli guy explained it to me. It's when something changes and part of it is lost. A bit like the food we eat, our body takes nutrients, transforms them into energy and expels the rest as... you know. Poo. So there's death but only in the context of transformation, of change. But I googled it and a baby name website said it just meant 'devoted to destruction' which is... well, a little worrying.

I'm a bit scared if I'm honest, Mum. I'd really like you to –

(*She looks at her phone. It has gone black.*)

Damn it!

(*She shouts into the void.*)

Anybody have a charger I can borrow?

(*She laughs and then she cries but not for long. She pulls herself together.*)

Bye, Mum.

'Saturday'

The Old Bachelor

William Congreve

Speaking directly to the audience, the Prologue introduces the audience the play. In this comedic speech, the actor forgets their lines.

PROLOGUE: How this vile world is changed! In former days
Prologues were serious speeches before plays,
Grave, solemn things, as graces are to feasts,
Where poets begged a blessing from their guests.
But now no more like suppliants we come;
A play makes war, and prologue is the drum.
Armed with keen satire and with pointed wit,
We threaten you who do for judges sit,
To save our plays, or else we'll damn your pit.
But for your comfort, it falls out to-day,
We've a young author and his first-born play;
So, standing only on his good behaviour,
He's very civil, and entreats your favour.
Not but the man has malice, would he show it,
But on my conscience he's a bashful poet;
You think that strange – no matter, he'll outgrow it.
Well, I'm his advocate: by me he prays you
(I don't know whether I shall speak to please you),
He prays – O bless me! what shall I do now?
Hang me if I know what he prays, or how!
And 'twas the prettiest prologue as he wrote it!
Well, the deuce take me, if I han't forgot it.

(*Runs off.*)

Prologue

Red Dust Road

Tanika Gupta, adapted from the novel by **Jackie Kay**

*Jackie (Nigerian Scottish heritage) is growing up in Scotland in the 1970s.
She is the adopted child of Helen and John. In this speech, sixteen-year-old
Jackie admires Angela Davis for her activism and bravery, whilst seeing herself
reflected in Angela.*

*(Jackie is in her bedroom reading. A poster of Angela Davis is hanging up. Jackie
kisses Angela Davis' face on the poster again and again and then steps forward.)*

JACKIE: On my bedroom wall is a big poster
of Angela Davis who is in prison
right now for nothing at all
except she wouldn't put up with stuff.
My mum says she's only 26
which seems really old to me
but my mum says it is young
just imagine, she says, being on
America's Ten Most Wanted People's List at 26!
I can't.
Angela Davis is the only female person
I've seen (except for a nurse on TV)
who looks like me. She had big hair like mine
that grows out instead of down.
My mum says it's called an Afro. If I could be as brave as her when I get older
I'll be ok.
Last night I kissed her goodnight again
and wondered if she could feel the kisses
in prison all the way from Scotland.
Her skin is the same too you know.
I can see my skin is that colour
but most of the time I forget,
so sometimes when I look in the mirror
I give myself a bit of a shock
and say to myself *Do you really look like this?*
as if I'm somebody else. I wonder if she does that?

I don't believe she killed anybody.
It's all a lot of phoney lies.
My dad says it's a set-up.

I asked him if she'll get the electric chair
like them Roseberries he was telling me about.
No he says the world is on her side.
Well how come she's in there I thinks.
I worry she's going to get the chair.
I worry she's worrying about the chair.
My dad says she'll be putting on a brave face.
He brought me a badge home which I wore
to school. It says FREE ANGELA DAVIS.
And all my pals says 'Who's she?'

Act 1, Scene 12

Level 1 Acting: Grade 3 Duologue

Alice in Wonderland

Jack Bradfield, Gerel Falconer and **Poltergeist Theatre**

After arguing with her Mum in Brixton station, eleven-year-old Alice runs onto the tube and is catapulted into a world of Nonsense. Alongside the other passengers, which include a Tortoise, Rabbit and Cat, Alice is at the mercy of the Queen who controls the train. In this scene, Alice and the Queen go head-to-head.

ALICE: Queen, Queen. Where are you?

(*A long and slow laugh.*)

QUEEN: You're supposed to be in the Gap.

ALICE: Show your face.

QUEEN: You don't give up, do you. Always breaking the rules, and rules are there for a reason.

ALICE: What... are you scared of the Overgrounder?

QUEEN: Scared, I'm not scared of anything.

ALICE: Let the Chatter drive!

QUEEN: I'm afraid I'm what the train needs right now.

ALICE: That's not TRUE.

QUEEN: Yes it is.

ALICE: No it's not.

QUEEN: Yes it is.

ALICE: Not it's not.

QUEEN: Stop, we don't do that here. Guards! Guards!! Guards?

ALICE: They're not coming.

QUEEN: Jabberwocky!
JABBERWOCKY.

(*Nothing.*)

Right. I see.

(*The Queen emerges. Alice draws her sword.*)

ALICE: You don't belong here, I'm throwing you in the Gap.

QUEEN: I don't want to do this Alice.

ALICE: We're *doing it.*

QUEEN: Very well. Prepare to meet your maker. Meet me on top of the train.

(*They step out on top of the train. Wind. Lights flashing past.*)

ALICE: You've been lying to us. You're sending us round in a loop. And you hurt my friends...

QUEEN: You don't know what you're saying.

ALICE: There's only one place for you.

QUEEN: And where's that Alice?

Sitting in your bedroom writing your lyrics?

(*Alice struggles to respond.*)

What are you saying? Use your English.

ALICE: JUST SHUT UP!

QUEEN: Guess this is a battle then.

ALICE: AAAAAAAAAAAAAAAA.

QUEEN: Don't get Osterley with me, you Croxley little flea.

ALICE: I'm a power station mate, I'll send you to Battersea.

QUEEN: I'll cut you in two like Highbury and Islington.

ALICE: I'll know you back and forth like it was in Wimbledon!

QUEEN: You'll be MaryleBONES when I'm finished.

ALICE: My Cutty Sark will leave you diminished.

QUEEN: X marks the spot so prepare for my Brent Cross.

ALICE: I'll give you the wry-slip.

QUEEN: I'll Fairlop your head off.

ALICE: I'll puncture your Paddington – my Stratford is red hot!

QUEEN: The train terminates here and you'll never get off!

(*The Queen gets the advantage. But then the digital Cat appears, and rings her phone.*)

One second I've got a notification... AH! CAT!

(*Alice fights back.*)

(*Shouting over the noise of the train.*) You just don't give up, do you?

ALICE: You're sending everyone in circles.

QUEEN: Well that's life isn't it! We're all going in circles.

(*They battle. Alice nearly falls off the train but regains her balance.*)

Careful!

ALICE: You're not my Mum! (*With every swing.*) STOP. TELLING. ME. WHAT. TO. DO.

QUEEN: I'm TRYING MY BEST.

ALICE: I HATE YOU.

(*Alice forces the Queen over to the edge of the train. She holds the sword over her.*)

QUEEN: Go on. Do it. Throw me in.

(*The Queen sniffles.*)

ALICE: What are you doing?

QUEEN: Nothing. I'm – I'm not doing anything –

ALICE: You're crying.

QUEEN: I'm not.

ALICE: You... are.

(*The Queen cries. Alice drops the sword.*)

Hey. Hey. What's wrong.

QUEEN: I don't know what to do. I'm just trying to keep everyone safe.

ALICE: Let's slow down. Let's stop.

QUEEN: No, we can't slow down, that's the problem. The train is BROKEN. All the controls are stuck. I can't change direction. It keeps speeding up and going round and round and round. I don't know what to do.

ALICE: Show me. I can help you.

QUEEN: I don't know if I can get up.

(*Alice reaches out her hand.*)

ALICE: *Hold my hand.*

(*The Queen grasps it.*)

Act 2, Scene 7

Wuthering Heights

Emily Brontë, adapted by LAMDA

Linton, the son of Heathcliff and Isabella, lives at Wuthering Heights with Heathcliff who mistreats him. When Cathy, the daughter of Catherine and Edgar, visits Wuthering Heights, she is keen to strike up a friendship with Linton despite his hostility and coldness. In this scene, Linton manipulates Cathy into feeling sympathy towards him.

LINTON: Is that you, Miss Linton?

(*Cathy runs towards Linton to give him a hug.*)

LINTON: No! You'll take my breath. Papa said you would call.

CATHY: Well, Linton –

LINTON: Will you shut the door, if you please? You left it open.

(*Cathy shuts the door.*)

CATHY: Are you glad to see me?

LINTON: Why didn't you come before? You should have come, instead of writing. It tired me dreadfully, writing those long letters. I'd far rather have talked to you. I want to drink.

(*Cathy searches for water.*)

CATHY: And are you glad to see me?

LINTON: Yes, I am. It's something new to hear a voice like yours! But I have been vexed, because you wouldn't come. And papa swore it was owing to me: he called me a pitiful, shuffling, worthless thing; and said that you despised me, Miss –

CATHY: I wish you would say Catherine, or Cathy.

LINTON: You don't despise me, do you?

CATHY: Despise you? No! Next to Papa and Ellen, I love you better than anybody living.

LINTON: But could you like me as well as your father?

CATHY: No! I should never love anybody better than Papa.

LINTON: *My* papa scorns yours. He calls him a sneaking fool!

CATHY: Yours is a wicked man. He must be wicked, to have made Aunt Isabella leave him as she did.

LINTON: She didn't leave him.

CATHY: She did!

LINTON: You shan't contradict me!

CATHY: She did!

LINTON: Well, I'll tell you something! Your mother hated your father.

CATHY: Oh!

LINTON: And she loved mine!

CATHY: You little liar!

LINTON: She did! She did!

CATHY: I hate you now.

LINTON: She did, she did, Catherine! She did, she did.

(*Cathy gives Linton a little push, causing him to fall. Immediately, he is seized by a violent cough. Cathy is stunned.*)

LINTON: Spiteful, cruel thing! I was better today: and there –

CATHY: I'm sorry I hurt you, Linton. But *I* couldn't have been hurt by that little push, and I had no idea that you could, either: you're not much, are you, Linton?

(*Linton does not respond.*)

Don't let me go home thinking I've done you harm. Answer! Speak to me.

LINTON: I can't speak to you. You've hurt me so, that I shall lie awake all night, choking with this cough! If you had it you'd know what it was: but *you'll* be comfortably asleep, while I'm in agony – and nobody near me. I wonder how you would like to pass those fearful nights.

CATHY: Must I go? Do you want me to go, Linton?

LINTON: You can't alter what you've done.

CATHY: Well, then I must go?

LINTON: Let me alone, at least. I can't bear your talking.

(*Cathy turns to leave.*)

CATHY: I dare not come again.

LINTON: You must come again, to cure me.

CATHY: No, I mustn't come, if I have hurt you.

LINTON You ought to come *because* you have hurt me: you know you have, extremely! I was not as ill when you entered as I am at present – was I?

CATHY: But you've made yourself ill by being in a passion. I didn't do it all.

(*Beat.*)

However, we'll be friends now. And you want me: you would wish to see me sometimes, really?

LINTON: I told you I did. Tomorrow, Catherine, will you be here tomorrow?

Chapter 23

Bright. Young. Things.

Georgia Christou

Sheara and Jasmine are twins and young geniuses. Their lives are completely in sync: they wear the same outfits, study the same subjects, eat the same meals. They are competing on TV for the Golden Brain trophy and the title of 'Britain's Brainiest Child'. In this scene, Jasmine and Sheara both reach the final round, but the competition is taking a toll on their relationship.

(*A corridor. Sheara is alone, looking at a book. Jasmine enters holding two brown bags.*)

JASMINE: There you are. Why are you skulking in a corridor?

SHEARA: I just wanted a minute on my own.

JASMINE: Two words. You're welcome.

(*Jasmine hands her a brown paper bag.*)

I had to beat Rochelle to the last cheese one so we could have the same.

(*Sheara takes the bag.*)

You're right, it's nice to be alone.

SHEARA: Jas, don't you ever get tired?

JASMINE: Told you we should have got to bed earlier.

SHEARA: No, I mean tired of this. Competing.

JASMINE: It's only one day.

SHEARA: It's *every* minute of every day.

JASMINE: What are you –

SHEARA: Why are you better at everything than me?

(*Beat.*)

JASMINE: I'm not.

SHEARA: First to walk. First to ride your bike.

JASMINE: You're talking rubbish.

SHEARA: We're meant to be the same.

JASMINE: We are. You just need more confidence. Don't worry so much about other people.

SHEARA: You mean don't make friends.

JASMINE: Friends like Rochelle?

SHEARA: She's nice.

JASMINE: She's obviously clever.

SHEARA: So?

JASMINE: So it's a bit suspicious, isn't it? How she just happened to be here at the right moment.

SHEARA: You just think everyone wants to win as badly as you do.

JASMINE: They do! Anyone who says different is lying.

SHEARA: That's not true.

JASMINE: You're honestly telling me, that you don't want this more than anything else in your entire life?

(*Beat.*)

(*Sheara picks the book up again.*)

JASMINE: We made it, Shear. The final.

(*Beat.*)

I thought you'd be happy?

SHEARA: Did you take it?

JASMINE: What?

SHEARA: Hester's mascot. Nelson's foot. Did you take it?

JASMINE: No. Why?

SHEARA: You made it clear you didn't like Hester.

JASMINE: I'm not a thief.

SHEARA: I was so sure. I told everyone you wouldn't do something like that.

JASMINE: Did Rochelle put this in your head?

SHEARA: You said it yourself. You want this more than anything else in the entire world.

JASMINE: I wanted both of us to get to the final.

SHEARA: Why?

JASMINE: Because...

SHEARA: Because you knew you could beat me?

JASMINE: No! The opposite.

(*Beat.*)

I'm going to let you win.

(*Beat.*)

I want you to get the trophy. You're always so hard on yourself. And you don't see how brilliant you are. You've been pulling away from me for months, Shear. I can't stand it. I just want everything to be how it was.

(*Beat.*)

SHEARA: *Let* me win?

JASMINE: I didn't mean...

Scene 15, 'Got You' – Scene 18, 'We Did It'

Maine Road

Sarah McDonald-Hughes

When fifteen-year-old Leo and seventeen-year-old Jade learn of the closure of Maine Road football stadium, they wonder what it means for Manchester City, the fans, and the community. Meanwhile, their grandmother dies. This scene takes place in their Gran's bedroom and explores Leo and Jade's grief.

(Jade and Leo look at each other. Jade grabs the letter again and reads it.)

LEO: What's it say?

JADE: It is very important that you contact West Area Housing Office immediately... Mrs Keenan did not alter the tenancy... there can be no succession... I would urge you to contact the office as soon as possible to discuss your rehousing options.

LEO: What's that mean?

JADE: I don't know. I'll have to ring them up won't I?

LEO: They can't chuck us out can they?

JADE: I don't know, do I? I'll ring them in the morning. Come on, Lee, help me get this tidied up.

(Jade goes to one side of the bed and straightens the covers.)

JADE: Get the other side.

(Leo helps Jade straighten the covers. Jade picks up the things from the bed and starts piling them neatly. Leo gets into the bed.)

JADE: What you doing?

LEO: I just want to get in a minute.

JADE: You're messing it all up again.

LEO: I'll make it again.

JADE: Leo –

LEO: Just one minute.

JADE: Alright – just while I sort this out then.

(*Pause.*)

(*Leo stares out the window.*)

LEO: That's why she had this room, you know.

JADE: What you on about?

LEO: So she could see it.

JADE: What?

LEO: Maine Road. Look.

(*They look out of the window.*)

JADE: Oh yeah.

LEO: Top of the Kippax, there.

(*Pause.*)

LEO: What do you think they'll do with it?

JADE: How do you mean?

LEO: Maine Road. What'll happen to it after Sunday?

JADE: They're gonna knock it down. Build something new.

LEO: At least Gran didn't have to watch them knocking it down.

JADE: Yeah.

(*Jade stands up.*)

JADE: Come on then.

LEO: Get in.

JADE: No!

LEO: Go on. It's nice.

(*Jade hesitates then pulls back the covers and gets in.*)

LEO: Smell.

(*They both breathe in the smell of the covers.*)

JADE: Gran.

LEO: How long will it last, do you think?

JADE: I dunno. A while. Maybe forever.

(*Jade breathes it in again.*)

Close your eyes and it's like she's here.

LEO: I wish she was here.

(*Jade looks at Leo. Leo doesn't look at Jade. Jade looks away again. They both stare out of the window, trying not to cry.*)

LEO: Imagine now, if she walked in and found us.

(*Jade laughs.*)

JADE: Sitting in her bed.

LEO: Smelling her covers.

JADE: She'd go up the wall.

LEO: Only allowed in Gran's bed when you're ill.

JADE: Yeah. And even then you have to lie dead straight so you don't mess up the covers.

LEO: And she tucks you in dead tight so you can't move.

JADE: Yeah.

(*Quiet.*)

JADE: Chips'll be cold.

LEO: I'm not hungry no more.

(*Pause.*)

LEO: Jade?

JADE: What?

LEO: They can't chuck us out of Gran's house can they?

JADE: No. I'll sort it out in the morning. Yeah? It'll be fine.

(*Leo lies down and pulls the covers round him. Jade does the same.*)

JADE: Lee?

(*Leo doesn't answer. Jade sits up again and tucks Leo in tightly.*)

Scene 4

Love and Information

Caryl Churchill

A and B are talking about pain. A is a child who does not know what physical pain is. B does not understand why A cannot feel pain. Therefore, B attempts to describe it.

A: But what is it?

B: Pain is pain, it's just

A: if I pinch

B: aah, get off. But if I pinch you

A: nothing

B: nothing at all

A: but stop because I get bruises.

B: How come you don't

A: I never did when I was a baby

B: you were born like

A: yes and I used to chew my fingers

B: you mean chew?

A: and they got bandages put over or I'd chew them to the bone because you know how babies

B: put everything in their mouth

A: I'd put myself in my mouth because it wasn't any different.

B: And if you fell down

A: I threw myself down

B: because it didn't hurt

A: jumped down a whole flight of stairs because that was a quick way

B: and you were all right

A: broke both my legs and once when I went swimming there were rocks under the water and when I came out my legs were pouring blood because I hadn't felt

B: so you can't feel anything

A: emotions I feel feelings

B: but physical

A: not pain, no.

B: And why not?

A: because there's no signal going up to my brain

B: from your legs

A: from anywhere to my brain to say there's damage, it's hurting

B: so you never know what hurting is

A: so tell me what it's like.

B: Hurting is well it's pain, it's like uncomfortable but more, it's something you'd want to move away from but you can't, it's an intense sensation, it's hard to ignore it, it's very

A: but why would you mind that?

B: because it hurts. But no, sometimes pain's all right if it's not bad like if your gum's sore and you keep poking it with your tongue or you might cut your finger and you hardly notice, yes if you're doing something exciting, soldiers can lose a leg and not even know it

A: that's like me

B: yes but they know it afterwards. And bad pain

A: yes but why, what is it?

B: if someone's tortured if they give them electric shocks it's unbearable or if they've got cancer sometimes they want to die because my uncle

A: yes but I still don't know what it is about pain

B: it's just pain

A: but what is it?

B: You've been unhappy?

A: yes

B: if someone you love doesn't love you, you thought they loved you and they don't

A: yes

B: or you've done something you wish you hadn't done it's too late now and you've hurt someone and there's nothing you can do to put it right

A: yes

B: does that help?

A: So it's like being unhappy but in your leg?

B: But it's also just what it is, like red is red and blue is blue.

A: But red isn't red, it's waves and it's red to us.

B: So there you are, that's what it's like.

A: Can I pinch you again?

Act 6, 'The Child Who Didn't Know Pain'

The Bone Sparrow

S. Shakthidharan, adapted from the novel by **Zana Fraillon**

Subhi is a male Rohingya in his early teenage years. Set in a detention centre in a remote Australian desert, Subhi has never set foot beyond the fences in which he was born. One day, he meets Jimmie, who comes from the other side of the fence. The pair share stories and their friendship grows. At the start of this scene, they give each other tattoos. It is Subhi's turn.

(*Jimmie passes Subhi the pen under the fence, then shoves her arm through. Subhi looks at Jimmie's arm.*)

SUBHI: Ouch.

JIMMIE: What?

SUBHI: That's a pretty bad scratch.

JIMMIE: Oh that? It's fine.

SUBHI: What happened?

JIMMIE: There's a nail sticking out from one of the drawers in my bedroom –

SUBHI: Oh! Did you show your dad?

JIMMIE: I'll show him on the weekend. Do you know what you wanna draw yet?

SUBHI: ...I think so.

(*Subhi begins tattooing her arm. The animations untether, fly and retransform.*)

(*As he draws.*) Jimmie?

JIMMIE: Yeah?

SUBHI: ...What's it like?

JIMMIE: What?

SUBHI: Your room.

JIMMIE: Like... a normal bedroom.

SUBHI: We live in a big tent. Our beds are made of steel. In those books Harvey brings me? None of the beds look like that.

(*Jimmie stares at Subhi, then nods, understanding.*)

JIMMIE: ...Well, I have my bed in the corner, so when I'm lying on it I can look out the window to our back garden and the washing line. I have two pillows on my bed and a photo of my mum on the drawers next to it. I have the dragon poster and... my school bag. (*Shrugs*) That's kind of it. And the walls are green.

(*Subhi soaks up every word.*)

SUBHI: When people here tell me their stories, they're from far away. Stories from other countries and other times. Stories of getting here. But no one has a story from just Outside. None of us knows what it's like just the other side of the fences.

(*Beat.*)

JIMMIE: I'll show you all over someday, Subhi, I know this place better than anyone. Near my house there's this paperbark tree full of pink galahs. They always come before the rains. And there's an abandoned mine with the biggest holes I've ever seen in it. You could see them from space! And there's a lake in the desert! A real lake! I followed the birds there. Someday I'll take you everywhere there is to take and we'll explore together everything there is to explore. I promise, okay?

SUBHI: ...Okay.

(*Subhi nods, overwhelmed. He finishes the tattoo. The animations show Islamic calligraphy, in the shape of a small person.*)

JIMMIE: (*Looking at it.*) What is it?

SUBHI: It's the word for patience, in Arabic. In the shape of someone waiting by a river, for their best friend.

(*Jimmie looks at it for a long beat.*)

JIMMIE: I love it. I'm going to take a photo and get it done as a real tattoo when I'm older.

(*Subhi's smile is as wide as the sky.*)

Thank you. (*Remembering something.*) Oh!

(*Jimmie gets a Thermos out of her bag and passes it under the fence to Subhi.*)

I brought some hot chocolate. Sorry. I know it's a stupid thing to drink when it's so hot but it's all I got.

(*Subhi just stares at it, gobsmacked.*)

Go on. It's for you.

SUBHI: Is this real?

JIMMIE: (*Laughing.*) What?

SUBHI: How did you manage to get hot chocolate?!

JIMMIE: (*Confused.*) What...? Oh. Have you never had it before?

SUBHI: I didn't even know it existed until a few days ago.

JIMMIE: Well... I'm glad I get to be here for the first time you try it.

(*Jimmie points at the Thermos.*)

Go on.

(*Subhi opens the Thermos like it's a sacred gift. He drinks slowly, but without stopping, for a long moment. Hot chocolate runs over the corners of his mouth.*)

(*Laughing.*) Guess you like it then?

.

SUBHI: (*Chocolate all over his face.*) ...All of life from now on is meaningless.

Act 2, Scene 1

A Midsummer Night's Dream

William Shakespeare, adapted by LAMDA

Quince, a carpenter, and Bottom, a weaver, are planning the performance of a play. In this scene, Quince is distributing the parts to each of the 'rude mechanicals'. Bottom wants to play every single part in the play.

QUINCE: Is all our company here?

BOTTOM: You were best to call them generally, man by man, according to the scrip.

QUINCE: Here is the scroll of every man's name which is thought fit through all Athens to play in our interlude before the Duke and the Duchess, on his wedding-day at night.

BOTTOM: First, good Peter Quince, say what the play treats on; then read the names of the actors; and so grow to a point.

QUINCE: Marry, our play is, 'The most lamentable comedy, and most cruel death of Pyramus and Thisbe'.

BOTTOM: A very good piece of work, I assure you, and a merry. Now, good Peter Quince, call forth your actors by the scroll.

QUINCE: Answer as I call you. Nick Bottom, the weaver?

BOTTOM: Ready. Name what part I am for, and proceed.

QUINCE: You, Nick Bottom, are set down for Pyramus.

BOTTOM: What is Pyramus? A lover, or a tyrant?

QUINCE: A lover, that kills himself most gallant for love.

BOTTOM: That will ask some tears in the true performing of it. If I do it, let the audience look to their eyes: I will move storms, I will condole in some measure. Now name the rest of the players.

QUINCE: Francis Flute, the bellows-mender? Flute, you must take Thisbe on you.

BOTTOM: Let me play Thisbe too. I'll speak in a monstrous little voice: 'Thisne, Thisne!' – 'Ah, Pyramus, my lover dear! thy Thisbe dear, and lady dear!'

QUINCE: No, no, you must play Pyramus; and Flute, you Thisbe.

BOTTOM: Well, proceed.

QUINCE: Robin Starveling, the tailor? Robin Starveling, you must play Thisbe's mother. Tom Snout, the tinker? You, Pyramus' father; myself, Thisbe's father; Snug the joiner, you the lion's part. And I hope here is a play fitted.

BOTTOM: Let me play the lion too. I will roar, that I will do any man's heart good to hear me. I will roar, that I will make the Duke say: 'Let him roar again; let him roar again!'

QUINCE: And you should do it too terribly, you would fright the Duchess and the ladies, that they would shriek: and that were enough to hang us all.

BOTTOM: I grant you, friends, if that you should fright the ladies out of their wits, they would have no more discretion but to hang us. But I will aggravate my voice so, that I will roar you as gently as any sucking dove; I will roar you and 'twere any nightingale.

QUINCE: You can play no part but Pyramus: for Pyramus is a sweet-faced man; a proper man as one shall see in a summer's day; a most lovely, gentleman-like man: therefore you must needs play Pyramus.

BOTTOM: Well, I will undertake it.

QUINCE: At the duke's oak we meet.

Act 1, Scene 2

Skunk

Zawe Ashton

Otto has big plans. He wants to ace his exams and play in a big game of football for all his fans. That's until one morning he wakes up to find he has turned into a skunk. His family are frightened of him, and no one wants to be near his smell. In this scene, Otto's sister Aaline brings him food.

(*Otto wakes up suddenly.*)

OTTO: Aaline?
Mum?
Dad!
Mum!
Dad!
Someone!
What time is it?
I'm late for school.
I didn't set my alarm again.
The sun's going down
I can see it through the trees. This room is turning into a forest,
There's a soft breeze picking up from underneath the door.
It's so quiet, you can hear ants and ladybirds move in the leaves and through the small patches of grass.
I'm a long way from home.
I'm a long way from home.

(*Aaline enters Otto's room without knocking. She carries a tray of food.*)

OTTO: Aaline –

(*Aaline is so scared of the sight of Otto she puts the tray of food down and runs out again. Otto goes to the food and sniffs it. Aaline takes a deep breath and re-enters.*)

AALINE: I didn't know what to bring.
Mum reckons you'll like vegetable peel so there's some of that.
I found a worm in one of Mum's window boxes.
There's some water and a Mars Bar – your favourite.
The Mars Bar, not the water.

(*Otto slowly crawls towards the food. He sniffs the chocolate but doesn't like it.*)

Don't you like Mars any more?

(*Otto shakes his head. He eats the vegetable peel messily and slurps the water. We see him eat the worm, Aaline grimaces.*)

OTTO: I'm so hungry.

(*He eats greedily.*)

You got any beetles? Any mice?

AALINE: Urgh! No.

OTTO: Sorry.
This is cool.
Thanks, sis.

(*Beat.*)

AALINE: There was a funny film on TV tonight about a family of aliens.

OTTO: I don't know what's happened, Aaline.
I don't know how it got this bad.

AALINE: It took them all ages to get used to their human bodies. You would have liked it.

OTTO: What are Mum and Dad saying about me?

AALINE: Mum and Dad are stressed.

OTTO: Because of me?

AALINE: I just think... it's a shock.
They'll get over it.

(*Beat.*)

OTTO: You scared of me?

AALINE: You're my brother.

OTTO: You know I'd never hurt you right?

(*Beat.*)

AALINE: Are you gonna change back?

OTTO: Yeah, course! I got a big game coming up, gotta be there for my fans!

AALINE: Idiot.

OTTO: And I can't miss the exams, so...

(*Beat.*)

You heard the one about the skunk?

AALINE: No?

OTTO: You don't want to –
It really stinks!

(*They laugh.*)

AALINE: How do you sleep? Can you reach your bed?

OTTO: I try but... these legs are shit.

AALINE: I can help you.

OTTO: No! Don't touch me! I might spray!

AALINE: That means you're scared of me. Mum says you do it when you're scared. Are you scared of me?

OTTO: Only of your face!

AALINE: Shut up!

(*She pounces on Otto, they play-fight and laugh.*)

(*Beat.*)

OTTO: I heard you singing earlier.
You sound good.

AALINE: I've started writing something new. Wanna hear?

(*Otto nods his head. Aaline sings 'Little Brother' by Ms Dynamite.*)

Otto?

(*Otto is fighting back tears he can't let Aaline see.*)

OTTO: That's good.
Needs some work.

AALINE: Shut up!

OTTO: Nah… it's really good.

AALINE: Thanks.
I'll make you a bed.

(*Aaline makes a small bed for Otto from pillows, a blanket and clothes. Otto lies down in the bed she made for him. Aaline strokes his head.*)

Goodnight, bro.

OTTO: Goodnight.

(*She exits.*)

Day 1, 'Night'

Daytime Deewane

Azan Ahmed

London, 1997. British Pakistani cousins Sadiq and Farhan are at a Daytimer. Daytimers were dance and music events that took place during the 1990s. Bunking school, second generation British Asians of all faiths came together in the afternoons, side-stepping their strict parents' night-time curfews, in response to racist club owners who wouldn't let South Asians in at night. Farhan is a hesitant dancer. Sadiq tries to help him forget about his Abu's potential deportation. Dance music fills the club.

SADIQ: Yo, I love this tune! Nice one Afshan! Come let's dance.

FARHAN: Can't.

SADIQ: Come onnn bro, let's show this room who the real peacocks are.

FARHAN: Nah, I…. it's time for me to go.

SADIQ: You just got here?

FARHAN: No. I know. Thank you. But I promised Abu.

SADIQ: He'll still be there when we finish.

FARHAN: He needs me now.

SADIQ: Of course Uncle is gonna need you. The butcher is gonna need you to buy his chicken. Mosque is gonna need you to fill space for jummah. Poor kids from the WaterAid advert are gonna need you to sponsor them…

FARHAN: Bro that's /

SADIQ: / Everyone will *need* you. But what do you need? Come on G: peacock energy.

(Farhan squirms, conscious of his familial obligations, and even more self-conscious of his dancing ability.)

FARHAN: Wait. Sadiq Bhai.

SADIQ: Yeah?

FARHAN: I just wanted to say... thanks for inviting me today. And sorry I was late.

SADIQ: Bro, we're family innit! Got your back; I know you'd do the same. Chalo, let's go!

FARHAN: Wait.

SADIQ: What now?

FARHAN: Can you show me it?

(*Sadiq looks puzzled.*)

SADIQ: What?

FARHAN: I can see it in your pocket cuz.

(*Sadiq becomes concerned.*)

SADIQ: What can you see?

FARHAN: Oh come on man, it's right there! I know you have one. Abu was telling me you bought it clean. I beg you show me I've never seen one before.

(*Sadiq is relieved, then amused.*)

SADIQ: Ohh, ok I see you eagle eyes.

(*Sadiq reaches into his pocket and takes out a flip phone. It's new. It's fresh. Sadiq holds the magical device up.*)

FARHAN: The Motorolla Star TAC?! Swear they're proper expensive?

SADIQ: Don't watch young blood, I make money moves innit – not confined to no classroom.

(*Farhan is mesmerised.*)

FARHAN: So you can call anyone, from anywhere?

SADIQ: As long as you got credit and signal.

FARHAN: Even Pakistan? Like Aunty Pasha and them?

SADIQ: (*Kisses teeth.*) Why am I gonna waste credit on them, all they're gonna do is ask when I'm getting married or when I'm going law school. I'm just doing me right now. Learning the law of the concrete jungle. You get me?

FARHAN: ...Nah not really...

SADIQ: How's Uncle?

FARHAN: Good.

SADIQ: Any luck on the /

FARHAN: Nah not yet, still appealing. Today's the – it's why I can't stay. Sadiq Bhai I shouldn't be here. I can't be doing all this madness while Abu is just sat there. He doesn't understand any of it. He gets so confused. I'm going.

(*Farhan makes to leave. Sadiq tries to stop him.*)

SADIQ: Woah, woah relax bro, we'll sort it, don't worry I got /

FARHAN: It's what you said right? See what you want and take it. I want to go home, so I'm going home.

(*Farhan is getting increasingly anxious.*)

SADIQ: Ok, I like the enthusiasm, quick learner, that's good. But listen – yo, listen! See how you're acting right now?

(*Sadiq puts his hand Farhan's chest.*)

Heart beating mad yeah? Hard to breathe? How's that gonna help your Dad? You walking in like some bull in a Chinese restaurant. I've got a surprise for you OK. Just one song and then you can go, you'll feel better, trust me.

(*Beat.*)

FARHAN: One more song... by the way it's china shop, not bull in a Chinese restaurant...

SADIQ: Huh??

FARHAN: Bull... in a china shop. Because China –

(*The music continues to play. Arm around Farhan, Sadiq starts to usher him towards centre stage for everyone to see.*)

SADIQ: Yo, I'm not discussing politics right now, and stop stalling! Come on.

(*Sadiq feels his phone vibrate in his pocket.*)

SADIQ: Yo, I gotta take this: hold tight yeah... You got this.

(*Sadiq slowly demonstrates a two-step.*)

SADIQ: One... Two... One... Two... yeah?

(*Farhan stays still. He looks at the crowd. Attempts a smile. Then a half-wave. Clears his throat. Attempts a two-step. He does it with the caution of someone stepping onto an ice rink, with socks on. Farhan, now two stepping slowly, looks at his legs. His lack of charisma annoys him. He looks at the Daytimer crowd, moving effortlessly, then back at his forced rhythm. Sadiq returns. Energised. He spots Farhan's very awkward dancing, but he's in a motivated mood to rectify this.*)

SADIQ: Oh. My. Days. Brudda? Come, come, come, come.

(*Sadiq continues to push Farhan onto the dance floor. They dance to the music.*)

Scene 6

Glossary: Urdu word (translation/explanation in English)
Afshan (the name of the DJ)
Abu (Father)
Jummah (Islamic Friday congregational prayer)
Bhai (brother: a term of respect for any older male relative)
Chalo (come on)

Flicker

Hannah Kennedy

Eve and May are siblings who recently lost their mother. They are at home and there is a storm outside. The power has just gone out. In this scene, they reflect on their grief, their love for their mother, and their love for one another.

(*Lightning. Thunder.*)

EVE: May! May?! May, the power's gone off!

(*May enters, brandishing her phone with the torch on.*)

MAY: You don't say! Don't we have candles?

EVE: I can't really remember where...

(*Lightning. Thunder.*)

MAY: Hold on.

(*May exits. A moment. May returns, brandishing three scented candles and a box of matches. May places them onto the ground and begins to light them.*)

EVE: What are they?

MAY: Candles?

EVE: No. I mean. What scent?

MAY: I think they're just vanilla?

EVE: Where did you find them?

MAY: In the bathroom.

EVE: Okay.

MAY: Why?

EVE: I don't know. Mum just never...

(*Lightning. Thunder.*)

MAY: What?

EVE: She never lit them.

(*Pause.*)

EVE: Said they were for guests.

MAY: What's the point of having candles if you're not going to light them?

EVE: I guess.

MAY: At least they smell nice.

(*Lightning. Thunder.*)

EVE: Have you ever done that thing where when there's a storm, you try and catch the moment that the thunder rumbles and the lightning flashes?

MAY: I don't know what you –

EVE: Like... uh, so you'd go...

(*Eve points to the sky. Nothing. Eve tries again.*)

EVE: It's not like doing it now, but... sometimes, when you're lucky, you'll point at just the right time, and it'll rumble and flash, and you'll feel like Zeus. It's more fun than... like, I'm explaining it. When I was a kid, I used to do it like, with the time. So, when it was like ten-fifty-nine or whatever, I'd try and point at the clock just as it would go to eleven, and it would make me –

MAY: Is there a point to this?

EVE: I guess not. I'm just trying to make conversation. We don't really, you know, have conversation...

(*Lightning. Thunder.*)

EVE: Missed it.

MAY: You do know you're not Zeus?

EVE: I know.

(*Eve points to the sky. Nothing.*)

EVE: I sometimes listen to the sound of storms to help me sleep.

MAY: And, yet, somehow, you've got no intention of sleeping right now, it seems. Seems like we're going to be up all night until the power comes on.

EVE: It's different when it's real.

MAY: How is it different?

EVE: There's just an electricity in the air.

MAY: It gives me a migraine.

EVE: Is that a thing? Do storms actually give people headaches?

MAY: It's either the storm or it's you. Why don't you shut up, and we can see which one it is? Or let's blow out the candles and go to sleep? The power will be on when we wake up.

EVE: I...

(*Eve blows out the candles. Points to the sky. Nothing. Eve tries again. Nothing.*)

EVE: I sometimes pretend that if I point to the sky and it thunders, then that means it's her. Telling me she's here. You know? Like, it's a sign. That she's here. You know, when you see those shows when people are like trying to get signs from ghosts, and they're like, I don't know, flicker this candle if you're here. I sometimes think that if I stand out in the storm and point my hands at the sky and it thunders then it means she's here.

(*Eve points to the sky. Nothing.*)

MAY: I used to think if I wished hard enough before I put the key in the door when I got home and turned the lock, that I'd push it open, and she'd be there.

EVE: Can I sleep in your room tonight?

(*Lightning. Thunder.*)

MAY: I miss her too.

EVE: You never talk about her.

MAY: I don't need to.

EVE: I'd like to talk about her.

MAY: I know you would.

EVE: Why don't you think you need to?

MAY: Because I'm not sad anymore.

EVE: Are you sure you're not sad?

MAY: Yeah.

EVE: Maybe you just don't know –

MAY: I'm not sad.

EVE: Okay.

MAY: I'm not sad all the time. Anymore. I'm not always sad.

EVE: But you're sometimes sad?

MAY: I think I'll always be sad, sometimes. Let's just... get some sleep?

EVE: Okay. Goodnight.

(*No reply.*)

EVE: May? Goodnight?

MAY: Goodnight, Eve.

(*Eve points to the sky. Lightning. Thunder.*)

Level 2 Acting: Grade 4 Solo

The Curious Incident of the Dog in the Night-Time

Simon Stephens, adapted from the novel by **Mark Haddon**

Christopher is very good at Maths. Prior to this speech, fifteen-year-old Christopher discovers a dead dog, investigates the death of the dog, discovers that his mother is not dead (as his father tells him), moves to live with her in London, and uncovers that his father killed the dog. Despite this, he passes his maths exam with an A*.

CHRISTOPHER: Thank you very much for clapping and thank you very much for staying behind to listen to how I answered the question on my maths A level. Siobhan said it wouldn't be very interesting but I said it was.

She didn't tell me what I should use, so I decided to use all the machines and computers in the theatre including: VL000 arc lights, which are moving lights, light emitting diodes, JBL control speakers, a Countryman boom mic and radio transmitter, 4 PTDX Panasonic overhead projectors and our DSM called Cynthia who will operate these.

I had ninety minutes to answer ten questions – but I spent thirty minutes doing groaning which meant I only had six minutes to answer this question.

Show that, a triangle with sides that can be written in the form n squared plus one, n squared minus one and two n (where n is greater than one) is right angled.

And this is what I wrote.

(*He runs and starts a timer.*)

Start the clock.

If a triangle is right angled, one of its angles will be ninety degrees and will therefore follow Pythagoras' theorem.

Pythagoras said that a squared plus b squared equals c squared.

To put it simply, if you draw squares outside the three sides of a right-angled triangle then add up the area of the two smaller squares, this will be equal to the area of the larger square. This is only true if the triangle is right angled.

Come on Bluey!

The A level question is an algebraic formula for making right-angled triangles. Algebra is like a computer program that works for whatever numbers you put into it.

To find the area of a square you must multiply the length by the width.

So... the area of this square is 2n × 2n.

Which equals 4n squared.

The area of this square is (n squared – 1) × (n squared – 1).

Which equals n to the power of four – 2n squared plus 1.

Then, if we add these two squares together ...

This equals n to the power of 4 plus 2n squared plus 1.

NOW... We need to find the area of square on the hypotenuse which is (n to the power of 2 + 1) × (n to the power of 2 + 1).

Which equals n to the power of 4 plus 2n squared plus 1.

Which is THE SAME TERM!

So the area of the two small squares adds up to the area of the larger square. So all my squares fit together to satisfy Pythagoras' theorem. So the triangle is – RIGHT ANGLED!

Quod. Erat. Demonstrandum

And that is how I go an A*.

Confetti.

'Maths Appendix'

Two Billion Beats
Sonali Bhattacharyya

Bettina, a fifteen-year-old British Asian girl, is being bullied by kids at school who charge her a 'door fare' to get on the bus. Bettina uses up all her birthday money to pay the bullies. Prior to this speech, Bettina's older sister Asha gives her a pep talk about how to stand up to the bullies. Speaking to Asha, Bettina recalls her success. She's ecstatic that she can finally save up for a pet hamster, Cardi.

BETTINA: I'm getting the bus. By myself. I'm getting the bus by myself. (*She pulls a five-pound note from her purse*) I can get on the bus waving this around. I can… (*She makes a neat triangle out of it and tucks it into the top pocket of her blazer.*) get on the bus like this. I can get on like –

(*Bettina jubilantly raps and/or sings a popular song about money. She knows all the words. She dances. She takes the opportunity to revel in this incredible victory.*)

I got on and they were like – (*Pretending to be Sana and Adeel.*) 'Here she is! Bettina, our queen! Yass! Saved a seat for you. Come over, babes.' And usually I'd try and front it out but this time I just acted how I felt. I was like 'Please don't hurt me. You can have my money if you want, but please stop hurting me. I can't take it any more.'

And first of all they started laughing, so I ramped it up. Started telling this lady next to me what they've been doing. (*Hamming it up.*) 'I was going to get a hamster but they've taken all my birthday money, and who knows what they've spent it on? And if my mum finds out she's going to kill me. I don't know what to do.'

(*Bettina pauses to make puppy-dog eyes at Asha, maybe even pretends to cry.*)

And this lady makes room on the seat next to her and has a go at Sana and Adeel, telling them they should be ashamed of themselves, and she'll call the police if they hassle me again, and how I'd be within my rights to call the police now if I wanted to, and maybe then they'd learn a lesson, because they obviously weren't learning anything at school. And the whole bus was bare quiet, and this lady gave me a Polo, and when we got to my stop the bus driver made a big show of stopping for ages, and getting out of his seat to wave me off and making sure Sana and Adeel didn't follow me.

It just all came out, yeah? Everything they've pulled for the past... what? Two months? Torturing me. Making life a living hell. So now I can start saving again and in a month I'll be able to bring Cardi home.

(*Beat.*)

I've got you to thank for this, you know?

No way I'd have been brave enough to do that if you hadn't prepped me.

Scene 4

A Woman of No Importance
Oscar Wilde, adapted by LAMDA

In the picture gallery at Hunstanton Chase, Gerald – a young clerk – is speaking to his mother Mrs Arbuthnot. Whilst Gerald is excited to receive a job offer to work as Lord Illingworth's secretary, his mother does not share the same enthusiasm. In this speech, Gerald tries to reason with her.

GERALD: Of course I am sorry to leave you. Why, you are the best mother in the whole world. But after all, as Lord Illingworth says, it is impossible to live in such a place as Wrockley. You don't mind it. But I'm ambitious; I want something more than that. I want to have a career. I want to do something that will make you proud of me, and Lord Illingworth is going to help me. He is going to do something for me.

(*Mrs Arbuthnot protests.*)

Mother, how changeable you are! You don't seem to know your own mind for a single moment. An hour and a half ago in the drawing-room you agreed to the whole thing; now you turn round and make objections, and try to force me to give up my one chance in life. Yes, my one chance. You don't suppose that men like Lord Illingworth are to be found every day, do you, mother? It is very strange that when I have had such a wonderful piece of good luck, the one person to put difficulties in my way should be my own mother.

Besides, you know, mother, I love Hester Worsley. Who could help loving her? I love her more than I have ever told you, far more. And if I had a position, if I had prospects, I could – I could ask her to – Don't you understand now, mother, what it means to me to be Lord Illingworth's secretary? To start like this is to find a career ready for one – before one – waiting for one. If I were Lord Illingworth's secretary I could ask Hester to be my wife.

(*Mrs Arbuthnot protests again.*)

You have always tried to crush my ambition, mother – haven't you? You have told me that the world is a wicked place, that success is not worth having, that society is shallow, and all that sort of thing – well, I don't believe it, mother. I think the world must be delightful. I think society must be exquisite. I think success is a thing worth having. You have been wrong in all that you have taught me, mother, quite wrong.

Act 3

I Am Yusuf and This Is My Brother

Amir Nizar Zuabi

In Palestine, January 1948, the British Mandate ends, and the United Nations vote on who will control what part of the land. War begins. Yusuf is a young Palestinian growing up in the village of Baissamoon with his brother Ali, surrounded by conflict. In this speech, Yusuf reflects on the war.

(Bullets whistle by.)

YUSUF: The south army is fighting the north army and the wind blows.
Where is everyone? Hiding in the bushes?
The leaves on the trees are fighting gravity and the wind is fighting the branches
And the urge to howl
Now the Army is attacking from all fronts!
The wheatsheaves fight against their ripeness and the hard working ants.
The stone walls of our houses fight the salt in our tears and the shrubs.
The rain is attacking tears
And the white of our bones bleaches the whiteness of the clouds...
Where is everyone? Running through the olive groves?
The tank is attacking the rice on our plates
And the bitter coffee in our tiny rattling cups.
The cows attack the grass and the grass gives shelter to the dead.
The sheep attack our wool coats and the shepherd on the cross.
And the donkeys resist forgetfulness with stubbornness.
The machinegun is spreading sesame on my grandmother's bread
And her warm greeting to a passing guest
Where is everyone? Hiding in the wells?
The airplanes are fighting the butterflies
And the silver mosquitoes swam round the eyes of the dead dog.
The hungry children bite off their elbows to attack their empty stomachs.
The marching army attacks the snakes in the fields with the stomp of their boots
And the hand grenade attacks the hands and the orange fruits on the trees.
Mice attack the flour sacks.
Flowers attack the graves.
Where is everyone? Hiding under their beds?
The bullets race the wasps and my heart is racing its galloping horses
And the pigeons swirl round the white flags that were my mother's dowry sheets
And the blushing blood of her purity is washed by the black blood of dead hens.

Where is everyone? Gone to the dust and the tents over the hills?
Where is everyone? Where are the smells of cooking food?
Where are the greetings and good mornings of the dawn?
Where are the villagers with their sourdough dreams?
Where is everyone? Am I alone? Has time ended?
Is it the beginning? When will it end?

Act 3, 'The Attack on Baissamoon – 25 June 1948'

Women Beware Women

Thomas Middleton

Isabella is the daughter of Fabritio, who arranges Isabella's marriage to the young and foolish Ward. Prior to this speech, Isabella has just seen the Ward and is not happy with the prospect of marrying him. She reflects on her position as a woman destined for an unhappy marriage.

ISABELLA: (*Aside.*) Marry a fool!
Can there be greater misery to a woman
That means to keep her days true to her husband,
And know no other man! so virtue wills it.
Why; how can I obey and honour him,
But I must needs commit idolatry?
A fool is but the image of a man,
And that but ill made neither. Oh, the heart-breakings
Of miserable maids, where love's enforc'd!
The best condition is but bad enough:
When women have their choices, commonly
They do but buy their thraldoms, and bring greater portions
To men to keep 'em in subjection;
As if a fearful prisoner should bribe
The keeper to be good to him, yet lies in still,
And glad of a good usage, a good look
Sometimes; by'r lady, no misery surmounts a woman's!
Men buy their slaves, but women buy their masters:
Yet honesty and love makes all this happy,
And, next to angels, the most bless'd estate.
That providence, that has made ev'ry poison
Good for some use, and sets four warring elements
At peace in man, can make a harmony
In things that are most strange to human reason.
Oh, but this is marriage!

Act 1, Scene 2

Dance Nation
Clare Barron

Zuzu is part of an American dance group led by Dance Teacher Pat. They are devising a new routine to perform at the Nationals, and thirteen-year-old Zuzu is auditioning for the role of Ghandi. In this speech, she reflects on her dance skills before her audition.

(*Zuzu alone.*)

ZUZU: People say I dance with a lot of grace and that I'm beautiful and above-average and stuff.
Here's what they don't say.
They don't say I'm sensational.

They don't say I take their breath away.
They don't say they could watch me forever.
They don't say they cry when they watch me dance.
When they watch Amina dance, they cry.
I know. Because I cry when I watch Amina dance.

My Mom asked me to dance for her cancer. She saw a documentary about this woman who did a dance and it cured her cancer and so she asked me if I would do a dance for her and my Mom is not normally like that but she was feeling really emotional at the time and she kept breaking down all the time so I did this solo at the year end recital for my Mom and her cancer. And I tried to make it the best dance I had ever done. I tried to like feel things with my arms and my legs. I tried to make people feel things with my arms and my legs... But it was just an ordinary dance, really. A lot of people didn't know it was about my Mom's cancer at all. They thought it was about whatever our dances are usually about. Flowers. Or sailors, you know. Not cancer. I didn't make them cry. I didn't make myself cry. I don't even think I made my Mom cry. She told me that she liked it. But she didn't cry. And it didn't cure her cancer, so. Her cancer actually got worse after that, so. It was just an ordinary dance.

Luke says I'm a genius dancer but he's lying to me because he's in love with me. Luke has dandruff. I know because I was playing with his hair the other day and at the base of his hair near his scalp were all these flakes of scalp sitting in his hair like dead ants that had just crawled out of a hole and died.

(*Zuzu dances the audition part for Ghandi. She's not that great.*)

Scene 5

The Two Gentlemen of Verona

William Shakespeare

Launce, a clownish servant, is speaking to the audience about his dog Crab. He describes how he takes the blame for all of Crab's mischief to protect his dog from being punished.

(Enter Launce with his dog.)

LAUNCE: When a man's servant shall play the cur with him, look you, it goes hard: one that I brought up of a puppy; one that I saved from drowning, when three or four of his blind brothers and sisters went to it. I have taught him, even as one would say precisely 'Thus I would teach a dog'. I was sent to deliver him as a present to Mistress Silvia, from my master; and I came no sooner into the dining-chamber, but he steps me to her trencher, and steals her capon's leg. O, 'tis a foul thing, when a cur cannot keep himself in all companies: I would have (as one should say) one that takes upon him to be a dog indeed, to be, as it were, a dog at all things. If I had not had more wit than he, to take a fault upon me that he did, I think verily he had been hanged for't; sure as I live he had suffered for't. You shall judge: he thrusts me himself into the company of three or four gentleman-like dogs, under the Duke's table; he had not been there (bless the mark) a pissing while, but all the chamber smelt him. 'Out with the dog!', says one; 'What cur is that?' says another; 'Whip him out', says the third; 'Hang him up' says the Duke. I, having been acquainted with the smell before, knew it was Crab; and goes me to the fellow that whips the dogs: 'Friend,' quoth I, 'you mean to whip the dog?' 'Ay, marry do I,' quoth he. 'You do him the more wrong,' quoth I; ''twas I did the thing you wot of.' He makes me no more ado, but whips me out of the chamber. How many masters would do this for his servant?

Act 4, Scene 4

Antigone

Lulu Raczka, adapted from the text by **Sophocles**

*In Thebes, the war has ended. Antigone and Ismene are sisters. Their brother
Polynices is dead and left outside the gates of the city. To bury their brother,
Antigone must rebel against her uncle King Creon, and break the law. Against
this backdrop, Antigone and Ismene dream of dancing, going out, and behaving
like teenagers. In this speech, Antigone speaks to Ismene about Haemon, who
she is in love with.*

ANTIGONE: Ismene.
I know.
But just listen.
So we think about each other
But we never write
And eventually we both forget about each other a little
Not properly –
But like that thing people always say happens
When you get old?
Where you kind of accept that your fantasies won't come true
And you accept reality
So we accept each other as just a dream
Something that's never going to happen
And move on with our lives
And so we fall in love with other people
And we marry other people
And we have kids with other people
But sometimes both of us wake up in the night
And think of each other
But we know it's just a dream
And we make an effort to forget about it
You know?
And get on with our days
But that memory
It won't go
We always find ourselves when we're with our actual
Husbands
And our actual wives
We find ourselves thinking
Is this right?
Would it be better with them?
That person I knew as a child?
And we look at our kids and we think

What would my kids be like
With that person I never got to know
How would they be different?
Would they be kinder
Funnier
Would I love them more?
But as you can imagine
This gets in the way of our lives
So anytime the thought comes up we both fight it
We say no
It's a dream
Move on
Grass is greener and all that
But then one day
I'm travelling
And he's travelling
And we're going down the same road
From different directions
And a deer runs into the road
And both of us have to stop
There's a crash
And we both walk into the road
Trying to work out what happened
And we both see this deer
But then we look up –
And I see this figure ahead
And he looks up
And he sees this figure ahead –
And neither of us can see much –
We're far away –
But we both get this feeling –
A feeling that says
I know this person
I maybe even know this person better than anyone I've known
For my whole life
And this person who I can't really see
This person knows me better
Than anyone else I've ever known.

Act 1

Nomad Motel

Carla Ching

Mason is a seventeen-year-old Hong Kong native (but passing as Asian American) living in Orange Country. Mason has been dropped off in the United States to go to high school and lives alone in a big house. Mason's mother has just died and his father has seemingly disappeared and stops sending money. Flat broke and fearing deportation, Mason sets out to apply to an American college with the help of his friend Alix. This is Mason's personal statement on his application, his hail mary at being able to stay in the States.

MASON: I scrapped the other one. This is from scratch. Okay.

(*Mason does that weird siren exercise every drama school teacher teaches their students in voice class.*)

Sorry. Vocal warm-up. We do it in debate.

(*Mason starts to read from his college essay. Mason's hands shake a little and the paper flutters.*)

You said a letter.

Dear Alix.

I don't want to go to college for the reasons most other people want to go to college.
Most people want to build the next big thing or be the next big thing.
Not me.

Most people want to earn five million Twitter followers, see their face on billboards, and demand that there be a bowl of white M&Ms wherever they go.
Not me.

My father wants me to go to Harvard so I can get an MBA and move a lot of money around.
Not me.

I'm not interested in being 'great.'
I'm not interested in being the Next Big Thing.
I'm just interested in doing the right thing.

Two months ago,
I found a dying bird.
We set its wing, fed it sugar water and nursed it back to health.
No one was watching.
We didn't Instagram it or Snapchat it.
We saved the bird and nursed it back to health because it was the right thing to do.

Music has done for me what the sugar water did for our bird.
She has nursed me back to health.
She has made me get stronger.
Music is the one language that doesn't plague me with her rules and rhythms.
But frees me to express everything that I am.
Wherever in the world I am forced to go, I have her, even when I have no one else.

I want not just to make music, but to teach music because music has saved my life.
Given me a home.
Given me a reason.
And I want to teach other people how to play.
To help them find a home. A reason. A voice.
To give them the tools to save their own lives when they have no one and nothing.
Because that's what greatness looks like to me.

(*Mason crumples the essay up and throws it aside. Embarrassed that it's all wrong. But Alix is incredibly moved. Upon hearing her voice, Mason's eyes brighten.*)

Are you sure? That's it? Really?

(*Mason picks up the crumpled essay and smooths it out.*)

Scene 12

A Doll's House

Henrik Ibsen, translated by **Kenneth McLeish**

*Nora is married to Torvald Helmer, a successful banker. Unknown to Helmer,
Nora has helped her husband out of a difficult financial situation by forging
her father's signature on a legal document. In this speech, she speaks to her
childhood friend Kristine Linde, explaining her actions.*

NORA: Well, Kristine? What d'you think of my great big secret? D'you still
think I'm silly? No cares in all the world? Don't think it's been easy, meeting the
payments on time, each time. Quarterly accounts, instalments – I can tell you all
about that sort of thing. Keeping up with them's not easy. I've saved a little bit
here, a little bit there. Not much from the housekeeping, because of Torvald's
position. The children couldn't go without nice clothes. Every penny he gave for
my little darlings, I spent on them.

Every time Torvald gave me money for clothes, I put half of it away. I bought
the simplest, cheapest things. Thank heavens everything looks good on me:
Torvald never noticed. But it was hard, Kristine, often. It's nice to wear nice
clothes. Don't you think? Fortunately there were other things I could do. Last
winter I was lucky: I got a lot of copying. I locked myself in every evening and
sat and wrote, into the small hours. It was exhausting. But it was thrilling too, to
be sitting there working, earning money. Almost like a man.

Business: it's hard to keep track of. All I know is, I paid every penny I could
scrape together. The number of times I didn't know how I'd manage! (*Smiling.*)
When that happened, I used to sit and daydream. A rich old man was head
over heels in love with me – Sh! He died, and when they read his will, there it
was in capital letters: ALL MY CASH TO BE PAID OVER INSTANTER TO THAT
DELIGHTFUL NORA HELMER.

(*Kristine is confused.*)

Heavens, can't you guess? He didn't exist, he just came into my head every time
I sat here thinking how to get some money. It doesn't matter now, anyway. The
silly old nuisance can stay away; I don't need him and I don't need his will. I'm
free of it! (*Jumping up.*) Free, Kristine, free of it! I can play with the children...
make the house pretty, make everything the way Torvald likes it. It'll soon be
spring, the wide blue sky. We could have a holiday... the seaside. Free of it! I'm
so happy, so happy.

Act 1

Level 2 Acting: Grade 4 Duologue

Glow
Manjinder Virk

Ant and Kul are best friends. Kul is a fourteen-year-old British Asian girl, and Ant is a fourteen-year-old Caucasian boy. In this scene, they are watching Pop Idol when one of their classmates from school appears on the television. This leads them to speak about their dreams: Kul wants to be a boxing champion, and Ant wants to be a hobbit.

(Ant's living room. Ant and Kul watch TV. The sound of 'Popstars'/'Pop Idol'. Someone is singing Christina Aguilera's 'Beautiful'.)

ANT: Oh my god, it's Tracey Ramsey.

KUL: What?

ANT: Oh my god, it's Tracey Ramsey!

KUL: No.

ANT: Oh my god! It's Tracey Ramsey!

KUL: Alright! I heard you the first time.

ANT: She's on telly, Kul!

KUL: It's easy to get on the telly, everyone does it.

ANT: Who do you know who's done it?

KUL: My Dad's friend... he did something about – a documentary about – you know, getting his house done and that.

ANT: What? Like 'Home Improvements'?

KUL: Yeah, that's the one.

ANT: I'd go on telly.

KUL: Who wants to see you on the telly?

ANT: Who wants to see you?

KUL: I never said I wanted to be on telly but I've got no choice but to live with it cos when I make it everyone's gonna wanna know me.

ANT: Yeah, sure.

KUL: I'll have em knocking my door down. I'll have to move somewhere far away so they don't know where I live, like the countryside or abroad. Like Posh and Becks. It'd be great. I'd have my own gym, won't have to go to school. I'd have money so I can do what I like. I can't wait. Don't look at me like that. You're lucky you got me as a mate.

ANT: I'm gonna get on telly.

KUL: Yeah – Telly Tubbies.

ANT: Ha ha.

KUL: You gotta do something to get on telly. You can't just be on telly for the sake of it.

ANT: Why not? Everyone else does it. Tracey Ramsey did it.

KUL: Did she win?

ANT: Dunno yet.

KUL: What's the point if you don't win? (*Beat.*) So what do you wanna do, Ant?

ANT: Dunno.

KUL: Not now – I mean what do you wanna *be*?

ANT: Dunno.

KUL: Dunno, dunno.

ANT: Why do you wanna know?

KUL: You jus' wanna get on telly?

ANT: I don't wanna.

KUL: But you said you did.

ANT: So?

KUL: You should learn to fight.

ANT: I'm alright.

KUL: I'll teach you some moves.

ANT: Nah...

KUL: I ain't always gonna be there to fight your battles.

ANT: I never ask you to.

KUL: You think I'm just gonna watch you get beat up. That time I saw you in the corridor when Dunks was trying to take your bag. If I didn't see him he would've laid into you, him and Calvin. And that time Kirsty and that lot started shouting, 'Cheesebreath...'

ANT: Alright, alright Kul!

KUL: No one messes with me at school.

ANT: Dunks and that lot call you names as well.

KUL: What have you heard them say?

ANT: It doesn't matter.

KUL: What?

ANT: They're just...

(*Beat.*)

KUL: Say it.

ANT: They're just racist, aren't they?

KUL: They wouldn't dare say anything to my face. You should learn to fight – you'll be alright then.

ANT: I want to be a hobbit.

(*Beat.*)

KUL: What?

ANT: Nothing.

KUL: You wanna be a hobbit?

ANT: Or a superhero.

KUL: You could be a hobbit, short arse.

ANT: It's like I disappear when I'm watching films. I'm in another world.

KUL: On another planet more like.

ANT: When I watch the telly I'm gone, I'm with Pat Butcher in the Queen Vic, with Vera Duckworth in '*Corrie*' but then Mum shouts to tell me my tea's ready and I know it's not real. The only time I really disappear is when I'm at the pictures, that's when I'm really gone. In another world with action heroes, superheroes, hobbits and wizards and anything that isn't me. In '*Lord of the Rings*', I was Frodo looking for peace and freedom for Middle Earth while under attack from the dark forces. 'One ring to rule them all'. I can be a hero. I love it – falling, riding, running, laughing, fighting – fighting with swords, fists, guns, fighting wars and adventures that go on forever, always getting the girl, having special powers, like going back in time or turning into a bird and flying, flying through the skies like Superman or jumping from buildings like Spiderman. It's magic and I love it, complete magic.

KUL: Yeah, well, it's not the same in real life. Life ain't got magic.

Act 1, Scene 5

Doctor Faustus

Christopher Marlowe

Faustus is a scholar who has become restless with the limitations of human knowledge. In his overambition and hunger for knowledge and power, Faustus turns to the study of magic and necromancy. In this scene, Faustus has conjured the devil Mephistophilis.

(*Faustus is conjuring. Enter Mephistophilis like a Franciscan friar.*)

MEPHISTOPHILIS: Now, Faustus, what wouldst thou have me do?

FAUSTUS: I charge thee wait upon me whilst I live,
To do whatever Faustus shall command,
Be it to make the moon drop from her sphere,
Or the ocean to overwhelm the world.

MEPHISTOPHILIS: I am a servant to great Lucifer,
And may not follow thee without his leave:
No more than he commands must we perform.

FAUSTUS: Did not he charge thee to appear to me?

MEPHISTOPHILIS: No, I came hither of mine own accord.

FAUSTUS: Did not my conjuring speeches raise thee? speak.

MEPHISTOPHILIS: That was the cause, but yet per accidens;
For, when we hear one rack the name of God,
Abjure the Scriptures and his Saviour Christ,
We fly, in hope to get his glorious soul;
Nor will we come, unless he use such means
Whereby he is in danger to be damn'd.
Therefore the shortest cut for conjuring
Is stoutly to abjure the Trinity,
And pray devoutly to the prince of hell.

FAUSTUS: So Faustus hath
Already done; and holds this principle,
There is no chief but only Belzebub;
To whom Faustus doth dedicate himself.

This word 'damnation' terrifies not him,
For he confounds hell in Elysium:
His ghost be with the old philosophers!
But, leaving these vain trifles of men's souls,
Tell me what is that Lucifer thy lord?

MEPHISTOPHILIS: Arch-regent and commander of all spirits.

FAUSTUS: Was not that Lucifer an angel once?

MEPHISTOPHILIS: Yes, Faustus, and most dearly lov'd of God.

FAUSTUS: How comes it, then, that he is prince of devils?

MEPHISTOPHILIS: O, by aspiring pride and insolence;
For which God threw him from the face of heaven.

FAUSTUS: And what are you that live with Lucifer?

MEPHISTOPHILIS: Unhappy spirits that fell with Lucifer,
Conspir'd against our God with Lucifer,
And are for ever damn'd with Lucifer.

FAUSTUS: Where are you damn'd?

MEPHISTOPHILIS: In hell.

FAUSTUS: How comes it, then, that thou art out of hell?

MEPHISTOPHILIS: Why, this is hell, nor am I out of it:
Think'st thou that I, who saw the face of God,
And tasted the eternal joys of heaven,
Am not tormented with ten thousand hells,
In being depriv'd of everlasting bliss?
O, Faustus, leave these frivolous demands,
Which strike a terror to my fainting soul!

FAUSTUS: What, is great Mephistophilis so passionate
For being deprived of the joys of heaven?

Learn thou of Faustus manly fortitude,
And scorn those joys thou never shalt possess.
Go bear these tidings to great Lucifer:
Seeing Faustus hath incurr'd eternal death
By desperate thoughts against Jove's deity,
Say, he surrenders up to him his soul,
So he will spare him four and twenty years,
Letting him live in all voluptuousness;
Having thee ever to attend on me,
To give me whatsoever I shall ask,
To tell me whatsoever I demand,
To slay mine enemies, and aid my friends,
And always be obedient to my will.
Go and return to mighty Lucifer,
And meet me in my study at midnight,
And then resolve me of thy master's mind.

MEPHISTOPHILIS: I will, Faustus.

Act 1, Scene 3

Heavy Weather
Lizzie Nunnery

After sixteen-year-old Mona has a panic attack in school following a science lesson on climate change, she is motivated to help the planet. Mona's mother, who she has not seen for three years, is pictured at a climate change protest, and Mona is desperate to track her down. In this scene, Mona is sitting on a coach next to an Influencer. Their differing world views become stark.

(The Influencer plonks down on the adjoining seat, holds up her phone and poses uncomfortably for a selfie. Mona's phone continues to beep through the following.)

INFLUENCER: *(To Mona.)* Could you just...? You alright to move over towards the window a bit? You're blocking the light.

MONA: The light?

(Influencer holds her phone high to get the rest of the bus in.)

INFLUENCER: Or actually, sit behind me. I'll just get the top of your head in over the seat. Make it look full in here.

MONA: *(Confused.)* I don't... I just...

INFLUENCER: *(Jumping up, looking out the window.)* Actually that's great. *(Snapping a photo.)* With the other bus outside and you just... sort of *there*.

MONA: Can I see?

INFLUENCER: It's only for my feed. You look fine. I mean you look... *(She looks Mona up and down.)* No one's looking at you.

MONA: *(Of the others on the coach.)* It's loud isn't it? I thought it'd be... I didn't think it'd be this...

INFLUENCER: Oh yeah it's fun. It'll be cool down there.

MONA: It *looks* cool. In the pictures. All the people. Everyone actually bothered and doing something and /

INFLUENCER: You get all kinds. I go for a classy 'on-trend city girl getting behind a cause' kind of thing.

MONA: You what?

INFLUENCER: Some of these people are a bit dated. Bit hippy. Bit hemp. All pale faces and second-hand clothes. (*Glancing awkwardly at Mona.*) Oh. Sorry. I didn't mean...

MONA: What didn't you mean?

INFLUENCER: (*Pulling out a lipstick.*) You want some?

MONA: I don't wear /

(*The Influencer grabs Mona's chin, applying the lipstick. Mona freezes, unable to protest.*)

INFLUENCER: It's all animal-friendly. Organic. Degradable materials. (*Holding Mona's face still.*) You're lucky – this is pre-release. Showed it on my channel yesterday.

MONA: Your channel?

INFLUENCER: You should subscribe. (*Still perfecting the lipstick.*) Beauty without guilt: who doesn't want that?

MONA: So you talk? And they hear you – loads of people?

INFLUENCER: (*Releasing Mona.*) Sort of. My followers are mostly super eco-conscious which is fab. It's *fab*. Just I've got to keep up. Got to turn up. Otherwise it's all comments, comments: 'Why isn't she saying this? Why isn't she doing that?' You know?

MONA: I wish someone listened to me. I wish I could speak /

INFLUENCER: (*Interrupting.*) And the sponsorship's gone crazy which is *so so* fab. But you know... it's all management. Managing the brand.

MONA: Which brand?

INFLUENCER: Me. (*Beat.*) But there's (*Using air quotes.*) 'me' and there's me. I'm the content so I've got to be sharp. Got to be on it. Always see how I'm seen. See how people see how I'm seen. You know what I mean?

(*Mona shakes her head, bewildered.*)

You've got to make sure you don't lose track. Make sure you don't fall in.

MONA: Fall in?

INFLUENCER: Click, click, click. Search your own name and you might never come back. You know?

MONA: I've got no idea what you're talking about.

INFLUENCER: It's fine (*Taking a photo of herself, checking it.*) It's fab. It's all fab.

(*Mona's phone rings over and over. Mona looks at it, indecisive. The Influencer watches.*)

INFLUENCER: Oh god, I get that... Exterminate you with a thousand rings and beeps. (*Making shooting gestures.*) Ping, ping, ping.

MONA: It's my big sister. She's /

INFLUENCER: Block her. That's what I do with my dad.

(*The phone rings again. Mona hesitates, stares at it.*)

Reading my texts. Hacking my email to check I'm not being groomed.

(*Mona silences the phone. It rings again, again. Mona silences it. It rings again and the Influencer grabs it.*)

I'll answer.

MONA: (*Grabbing for the phone.*) Don't.

INFLUENCER: (*Holding it high.*) Come on, it's funny.

MONA: Please. Just /

INFLUENCER: I'll tell her to disappear.

MONA: Just give it back.

(*Mona makes another grab. She and the Influencer fight over the phone. The Influencer laughs, struggles. Impulsively the Influencer chucks the phone away from Mona. They both stare out the window in shock.*)

INFLUENCER: Where'd it go?

MONA: What d'you mean? What d'you mean 'where'd it go'?

INFLUENCER: Sorry.

MONA: It went out... It went...

INFLUENCER: Sorry. Sorry, alright?

MONA: (*Moving close.*) That doesn't break down.

INFLUENCER: You can use my phone. You can have it. I've got three.

MONA: That won't go away.

INFLUENCER: Alright, calm.

MONA: No. No /

INFLUENCER: It's just a phone.

MONA: (*Leaning in, speaking close to her face.*) Animals will come in to the cities. Ice will melt in the mountains and the sun will dry up the forests. Bears and wolves will come in packs through the streets. That's how we'll know it's too late. And then the floods'll come. The ground'll belch centuries of sewage and landfill – and *that phone* will be riding high on a roaring tide of floating trash.

It won't break down. It won't go away.

(*The Influencer backs away, stares at Mona, terrified.*)

INFLUENCER: It was an accident, alright?

MONA: Everything's an accident. The whole human race is one big stupid accident – does that make it okay?

INFLUENCER: Weirdo.

Scene 2, 'Mona and the Influencer'

Fast
Fin Kennedy

Cara and Kirsty are siblings, living on a farm in a semi-rural town. Recently, their father died from suicide. At school, Cara is taking part in a twenty-four-hour fast to raise money for Oxfam. This scene takes place the night before the fast is due to begin.

Content warning: this scene references restricted eating and suicide.

(*Kirsty and Cara open a dictionary each, which becomes a dinner plate. They take out a knife and fork from a compartment in the middle. Cara picks at her food but doesn't eat.*)

KIRSTY: We had a viewing today.

(*Cara doesn't answer.*)

They were from a big chain. Industrial farming.

(*Pause.*)

The agent reckons they're serious.

(*Pause.*)

You should be pleased. If we can sell this place we might both get to go to uni.

CARA: One of the chickens has gone missing.

KIRSTY: Really? I don't know them all like you do.

CARA: It was Dad's favourite. The Amber White. The one with the red spot.

KIRSTY: You should eat.

CARA: I'm not hungry.

KIRSTY: Don't you like it?

CARA: No, I'm just not hungry.

KIRSTY: You're never hungry.

CARA: Can't help that, can I?

KIRSTY: You used to have a massive appetite.

CARA: Yeah, well, not any more.

KIRSTY: Tomorrow's the fast.

CARA: So?

KIRSTY: So you need to stock up.

CARA: Twenty-four hours is nothing.

KIRSTY: You'll be weak.

CARA: I've gone longer than that before.

KIRSTY: You've got revision.

CARA: Would you stop nagging me?

(*Pause.*)

KIRSTY: This asparagus is Dad's. He planted it. It takes three years to grow.

(*Cara gets up.*)

Where you going?

CARA: Upstairs.

(*She goes upstairs. She mimes opening a door and walking into a room.*)

(*To audience.*) Mum and Dad's room's at the top of the house, looking out over the farm. Well, it's just Mum's room now. But Dad's wardrobe is still in the corner. Big. Solid. Like him.

(*Cara opens the wardrobe.*)

Still full of his clothes.

(*Cara takes out a large winter jumper. Pulls it over her head and puts it on. It is way too big. Cara hugs it to her.*)

Still got his smell.

(*Cara breathes it in. She cries.*)

Miss him.

(*She gets angry.*)

But hate him.

(*She violently pulls the jumper off.*)

Miss him but hate him but miss him but hate him!

(*She flings the jumper into the wardrobe. It dislodges a shoebox which falls out. Letters spill onto the floor. She picks them up.*)

What the hell – ?

(*She reads some of them.*)

Oh my God.

(*Kirsty enters.*)

KIRSTY: You alright?

CARA: Have you seen these?

KIRSTY: What are you doing in here?

CARA: Letters.

KIRSTY: Cara –

CARA: From Dad. From Dad to his clients.

KIRSTY: Look –

CARA: Tesco, Morrisons, Asda.

KIRSTY: Your dinner's getting cold.

(*Cara reads one of them out.*)

CARA: 'Dear Asda head office, I enclose my farm's accounts for the last financial year. As you will see, for the third year running, it made a heavy loss, driving my business further into debt –'

KIRSTY: Cara –

CARA: 'Your company's 'price promise' to customers does not appear to be coming out of your profits. It is coming out of mine.'

KIRSTY: Alright, Cara, just stop.

CARA: There's hundreds of them –

KIRSTY: It's private.

CARA: To all the supermarkets he supplied.

KIRSTY: It's just old work letters.

CARA: Stretching back years –

KIRSTY: You shouldn't have read them.

CARA: He's dead, Kirsty.

KIRSTY: Then all the more reason!

CARA: But they all say the same thing! 'I'm struggling', 'You're driving me into debt', 'I've got two daughters who want to go to university'.

KIRSTY: Farming's hard –

CARA: Not this hard.

KIRSTY: – everyone knows that.

CARA: But this is why he did it, Kirsty! This is why he killed himself!

(*Pause.*)

KIRSTY: We don't know that, Cara. Nobody does. That's what happens when they don't leave a note.

CARA: (*Of the letters.*) Well, maybe this is his note.

KIRSTY: Come down. Eat your dinner.

CARA: You know what? I never want to eat again.

(*Cara storms off. Kirsty flicks through the letters.*)

The Tempest
William Shakespeare

Miranda lives on an island with her father Prospero, the exiled Duke of Milan. Miranda is isolated aside from her father and the magical creatures that inhabit the island. When Ferdinand is shipwrecked on the shore of the island, Miranda meets him and they immediately fall in love.

MIRANDA: Alas now, pray you,
Work not so hard. I would the lightning had
Burnt up those logs that you are enjoined to pile!
Pray set it down and rest you. When this burns,
'Twill weep for having wearied you. My father
Is hard at study; pray now, rest yourself.
He's safe for these three hours.

FERDINAND: O most dear mistress,
The sun will set before I shall discharge
What I must strive to do.

MIRANDA: If you'll sit down,
I'll bear your logs the while. Pray give me that;
I'll carry it to the pile.

FERDINAND: No, precious creature,
I had rather crack my sinews, break my back,
Than you should such dishonour undergo
While I sit lazy by.

MIRANDA: It would become me
As well as it does you, and I should do it
With much more ease, for my good will is to it,
And yours it is against.

MIRANDA: You look wearily.

FERDINAND: No, noble mistress, 'tis fresh morning with me
When you are by at night. I do beseech you –
Chiefly that I might set it in my prayers –
What is your name?

MIRANDA: Miranda. – O my father,
I have broke your hest to say so!

FERDINAND: Admired Miranda!
Indeed the top of admiration, worth
What's dearest to the world! Full many a lady
I have eyed with best regard, and many a time
Th' harmony of their tongues hath into bondage
Brought my too diligent ear. For several virtues
Have I liked several women; never any
With so full soul but some defect in her
Did quarrel with the noblest grace she owed
And put it to the foil. But you, O you,
So perfect and so peerless, are created
Of every creature's best!

MIRANDA: I do not know
One of my sex, no woman's face remember –
Save, from my glass, mine own. Nor have I seen
More that I may call men than you, good friend,
And my dear father. How features are abroad
I am skilless of, but by my modesty
(The jewel in my dower), I would not wish
Any companion in the world but you,
Nor can imagination form a shape,
Besides yourself, to like of. But I prattle
Something too wildly, and my father's precepts
I therein do forget.

FERDINAND: I am, in my condition,
A prince, Miranda; I do think a king
(I would not so!) and would no more endure
This wooden slavery than to suffer
The flesh-fly blow my mouth! Hear my soul speak:
The very instant that I saw you did
My heart fly to your service, there resides
To make me slave to it, and for your sake
Am I this patient log-man.

MIRANDA: Do you love me?

FERDINAND: O heaven, O earth, bear witness to this sound,
And crown what I profess with kind event
If I speak true; if hollowly, invert
What best is boded me to mischief! I,
Beyond all limit of what else i'th' world,
Do love, prize, honour you.

MIRANDA: I am a fool
To weep at what I am glad of.

Act 3, Scene 1

Everybody's Talking About Jamie: Teen Edition

Tom MacRae and **Dan Gillespie Sells**

Jamie is a teenager who lives in Sheffield and dreams of being onstage as a drag queen. Jamie's drag queen persona is called 'Mimi Me'. Pritti is Jamie's best friend, who faces bullying at school for being Muslim. Prior to this scene, Jamie has been told not to wear a dress to the school prom. Jamie goes to Pritti's house for support.

(Pritti's room is tidy, ordered and full of books. Instead of pin-up boys, she has maps of the world and historical figures. Pritti sits on her bed as Jamie paces the room.)

JAMIE: 'Disgusting'! How could she call Mimi Me 'disgusting'?! Mimi is gorgeous, and glamorous – and look at Miss Hedge in her knock-off Jimmy Choos – she's just jealous, she is! She *wishes* she was Mimi Me!

PRITTI: Jamie! Calm down! My mum and dad'll hear you – I'm not meant to have boys in my room.

JAMIE: Oh I'm sorry, please hold me back whilst I try not to ravish you.

PRITTI: Jamie! House rules! Come on!

(Jamie sighs, then sits on the bed next to her. Pause.)

JAMIE: Your room's so tidy, I don't know how you do it.

PRITTI: I don't have as many dresses as you do.

JAMIE: I like your lamp.

PRITTI: Thanks.

(Pause.)

Jamie, do you think... Miss Hedge maybe has a point? You are a bit... you know... of a... drama queen?

JAMIE: I am so *not* a drama queen!!!

(*Pritti raises an eyebrow.*)

...Fine.

PRITTI: I'm not saying I'm on her side, but she is right about one thing – prom in't just about you.

JAMIE: I wasn't making it about me!

PRITTI: Jamie – your dress is self-illuminating!

JAMIE: No! That's *Mimi Me!* That's how she dresses!

PRITTI: Why does Mimi Me have to be part of the equation?! I'm gonna be a doctor – it doesn't mean I have to go everywhere swinging my stethoscope. Why not just wear something simple to prom? Something modest. Not a drag queen, but a really beautiful boy.

JAMIE: There's nothing beautiful about me.

PRITTI: Jamie... you are *stunning*.

(*Beat.*)

You know, you've never asked me why I wear a hijab.

JAMIE: I know why – cos of your dad.

PRITTI: No! You see Jamie – sometimes you forget that other people... we're not all just your backing singers. You've never asked me – so go on, ask.

JAMIE: Why do you wear a hijab?

PRITTI: Because I want to. Because it keeps me simple. Because it frames who I am.

JAMIE: Are you saying... I should wear a burka?

PRITTI: No! I'm saying... don't go there to put on a show. Just go there as *you.*

JAMIE: But without *her*... I'm just ugly.

(*Pause.*)

PRITTI: You know there's a name like Jamie in Arabic: Jamil. So if you were Pakistani or Middle Eastern or whatever, they'd call you Jamil New –

And you know what Jamil means? It means beautiful.

JAMIE: One day, when I were eight, me dad come home early from work, and he caught me dressing up. It were this old thing of me mum's, sierra gold, this maxi dress, it was way too long for me so I'd sort of tied it in a knot at the side and I was swishing it about and lip-syncing along to Patsy Cline, like you do, and there he was, you know, just stood in the doorway, just staring at me... the look on his face... and he said... well *what* he said has made me feel ugly me entire life.

PRITTI: But he sent you the card and the flowers to your show. He paid for your dress. I mean it's strange in't it? Don't you think Jamie? It's strange.

(*She has an inkling of the truth.*)

JAMIE: I guess.

PRITTI: I think you should go and talk to him.

JAMIE: Yeah, maybe.

PRITTI: You could go now. Not that I'm trying to get rid of your or 'owt.

(*Jamie goes to leave, then pauses.*)

JAMIE: If I don't say it enough – you are the best friend a boy who sometimes wants to be a girl could ever ask for.

Act 2, Scene 4, 'Pritti's Bedroom'

The Importance of Being Earnest
Oscar Wilde

Jack Worthing and his best friend Algernon Moncrieff masquerade as a man named 'Ernest'. Jack is in love with Gwendolen, and Algernon is in love with Cecily. Jack and Algernon express their affections for Gwendolen and Cecily respectively, and both women fall in love with 'Ernest'. In this scene, Cecily and Gwendolen meet and reveal their engagements to 'Ernest'.

CECILY: (*Rather shy and confidingly.*) Dearest Gwendolen, there is no reason why I should make a secret of it to you. Our little county newspaper is sure to chronicle the fact next week. Mr Ernest Worthing and I are engaged to be married.

GWENDOLEN: (*Quite politely, rising.*) My darling Cecily, I think there must be some slight error. Mr Ernest Worthing is engaged to me. The announcement will appear in the *Morning Post* on Saturday at the latest.

CECILY: (*Very politely, rising.*) I am afraid you must be under some misconception. Ernest proposed to me exactly ten minutes ago. (*Shows diary.*)

GWENDOLEN: (*Examines diary through her lorgnettte carefully.*) It is certainly very curious, for he asked me to be his wife yesterday afternoon at 5.30. If you would care to verify the incident, pray do so. (*Produces diary of her own.*) I never travel without my diary. One should always have something sensational to read in the train. I am so sorry, dear Cecily, if it is any disappointment to you, but I am afraid I have the prior claim.

CECILY: It would distress me more than I can tell you, dear Gwendolen, if it caused you any mental or physical anguish, but I feel bound to point out that since Ernest proposed to you he clearly has changed his mind.

GWENDOLEN: (*Meditatively.*) If the poor fellow has been entrapped into any foolish promise I shall consider it my duty to rescue him at once, and with a firm hand.

CECILY: (*Thoughtfully and sadly.*) Whatever unfortunate entanglement my dear boy may have got into, I will never reproach him with it after we are married.

GWENDOLEN: Do you allude to me, Miss Cardew, as an entanglement? You are presumptuous. On an occasion of this kind it becomes more than a moral duty to speak one's mind. It becomes a pleasure.

CECILY: Do you suggest, Miss Fairfax, that I entrapped Ernest into an engagement? How dare you? This is no time for wearing the shallow mask of manners. When I see a spade I call it a spade.

GWENDOLEN: (*Satirically.*) I am glad to say that I have never seen a spade. It is obvious that our social spheres have been widely different.

(*A long pause. Cecily and Gwendolen glare at each other.*)

GWENDOLEN: Are there many interesting walks in the vicinity, Miss Cardew?

CECILY: Oh! yes! a great many. From the top of one of the hills quite close one can see five counties.

GWENDOLEN: Five counties! I don't think I should like that; I hate crowds.

CECILY: (*Sweetly.*) I suppose that is why you live in town?

(*Gwendolen bites her lip and beats her foot nervously with her parasol.*)

GWENDOLEN: (*Looking round.*) Quite a well-kept garden this is, Miss Cardew.

CECILY: So glad you like it, Miss Fairfax.

GWENDOLEN: I had no idea there were any flowers in the country.

CECILY: Oh, flowers are as common here, Miss Fairfax, as people are in London.

GWENDOLEN: Personally I cannot understand how anybody manages to exist in the country, if anybody who is anybody does. The country always bores me to death.

CECILY: Ah! This is what the newspapers call agricultural depression, is it not? I believe the aristocracy are suffering very much from it just at present. It is almost an epidemic amongst them, I have been told. May I offer you some tea, Miss Fairfax?

GWENDOLEN: (*With elaborate politeness.*) Thank you. (*Aside.*) Detestable girl! But I require tea!

CECILY: (*Sweetly.*) Sugar?

GWENDOLEN: (*Superciliously.*) No, thank you. Sugar is not fashionable any more.

(*Cecily looks angrily at her, takes up the tongs and puts four lumps of sugar into the cup.*)

CECILY: (*Severely.*) Cake or bread and butter?

GWENDOLEN: (*In a bored manner.*) Bread and butter, please. Cake is rarely seen at the best houses nowadays.

(*Cecily cuts a very large slice of cake, and puts it on the tray. Gwendolen drinks the tea and makes a grimace. Puts down cup at once, reaches out her hand to the bread and butter, looks at it, and finds it is cake. Rises in indignation.*)

GWENDOLEN: You have filled my tea with lumps of sugar, and though I asked most distinctly for bread and butter, you have given me cake. I am known for the gentleness of my disposition, and the extraordinary sweetness of my nature, but I warn you, Miss Cardew, you may go too far.

CECILY: (*Rising.*) To save my poor, innocent, trusting boy from the machinations of any other girl there are no lengths to which I would not go.

GWENDOLEN: From the moment I saw you I distrusted you. I felt that you were false and deceitful. I am never deceived in such matters. My first impressions of people are invariably right.

CECILY: It seems to me, Miss Fairfax, that I am trespassing on your valuable time. No doubt you have many other calls of a similar character to make in the neighbourhood.

Act 2

Gone Too Far!

Bola Agbaje

Yemi (aged sixteen, black) and Ikudayisi (aged eighteen, black) are brothers from different continents. Ikudayisi is proud of his heritage and can speak Yoruba, but Yemi cannot. In this scene, Ikudayisi tries to encourage Yemi to connect with his heritage but is met with resistance. As their conversation escalates into an argument, the differences between them become clear.

IKUDAYISI: I'm proud of who I am.

(*He sings.*)

Green white green on my chest,
I'm proud to be a Nigerian!
Green white green on my chest,
I'm proud to be a Nigerian!

YEMI: Oh my dayz!

IKUDAYISI: Green white green on my chest, I'm proud to be a Nigerian!

YEMI: Do you not see how stupid you look?

IKUDAYISI: Green white green on my chest, I'm proud to be a Nigerian!

(*He falls to his knees with his hands in the air.*)

Proud to be a Nigerian,
Proud to be a Nigerian,
Proud – to – be – a – Ni-ge-ri-an,
Proud – to – be – a – Ni-ge-ri-an!

YEMI: But then you put on a fake American accent when you talking to other people. (*Ikudayisi stops singing.*)

IKUDAYISI: That is just my accent, it is always changing.

YEMI: No. (*He mimics Ikudayisi's accent*) This is your accent. (*He mimics Ikudayisi's fake American accent*) And this is you when you're trying to be American. They are two different accents.

IKUDAYISI: I'm still proud to be Nigerian.

YEMI: You're telling me I'm lost, but what bout you? You can stand here all day going on bout how proud you are, but the truth is in your action, not just your word.

IKUDAYISI: Jo, leave me.

YEMI: Ohh, did I hit a raw nerve? Don't worry – as I said, your accent a joke, everyone understands why you want to get rid. It's no big ting. No one ain't gonna hate you if you change – I've already told you, I think you need to!

IKUDAYISI: You are so young, you don't understand anything at all. I was once like you. As I keep on saying, I just wish you went to Nigeria. The way you are talking you will see –

YEMI: I don't *wanna* go there.

IKUDAYISI: That's your problem, and why I personally feel sorry for you. You are telling me I need to change, but I'm not the one with the problem, it's you. You are a lost puppy. One minute you feel you don't fit in here because people are racist but then you don't want to be a Nigerian. Then you want to be left alone, but you complain you have no friend. Do you know who you are, Yemi?

YEMI: Yes, I'm a free person.

IKUDAYISI: Nobody is free-oh.

YEMI: You might not be, but I am.

IKUDAYISI: How can you be free when you deny your own heritage? You don't like your name, you are ashamed of your language. If you are so free you won't care what people think about Nigerian and you will just be what you are.

YEMI: Do you think I care what people think? It's not other people that make me hate Nigeria, it's Nigeria that makes me hate it.

IKUDAYISI: *But you have never been there.* How can you judge? Nigeria is a nice place.

YEMI: Forget it, man. You're not going to make me change my mind overnight. Let's go.

IKUDAYISI: No, ah ah.

YEMI: I don't care bout Nigeria. Why can't you just leave it?

IKUDAYISI: YOU NEED TO LEARN TO RESPECT IT! What are you going to teach your children?

YEMI: THAT THEY ARE FREE LIKE ME.

IKUDAYISI: And when they want to know about their family?

YEMI: This is long, man, lauw da chat.

IKUDAYISI: No. Will you even give your kids Yoruba names?

YEMI: I don't care.

IKUDAYISI: WELL, YOU SHOULD!

YEMI: Why? Why should I? I'm not you, I'm my own person. Stop trying to force your views on me. I'm sick of this. I just wanna be me. Don't wanna be no one else. Let me be me. Why do you care what I think?

IKUDAYISI: You *really* don't understand. Despite all its problem, Nigeria is a great place. YOU HAVE TO BE PROUD OF WHERE YOU ARE FROM.

YEMI: If it's so great, why do you *all* wanna come here?

(*Ikudayisi remains silent.*)

YEMI: *Exactly!* No matter how bad this country is, I bet it better than there!

IKUDAYISI: *Ironi yen.* [A lie.]

(*Yemi cuts his eye at Ikudayisi and kisses his teeth.*)

IKUDAYISI: I don't understand you at all. If people saw us now they would not even know we are from the same mother. We are brothers, and you act like we are from different countries, different worlds.

YEMI: We are.

Act 1, Scene 6

The Maladies

Carmen Nasr

In Tanzania 1962, a schoolgirl's laughing fit spreads from village to village. Academics deem it 'abnormal emotional behaviour', and issue guidance to parents on preventing their daughters from laughing. Susan and Christina are impacted. In this scene, they try their hardest to stifle their laughter.

(*Susan and Christina are listening to the radio, which has been playing the 'Advice to Tanzanian Mothers' public broadcast. Susan leans over and turns it off.*)

CHRISTINA: Why won't you look at me?

SUSAN: I told you. I can't.

CHRISTINA: Why?

SUSAN: You know who the stupidest and saddest people in the world are?

CHRISTINA: Old people?

SUSAN: No. Our mums and our aunties. They're the saddest and stupidest people. Ever.

CHRISTINA: My mum's not sad.

SUSAN: Even the radio tells them what to do. An object is more powerful than them. That's sad. They're losers. Our mums are losers.

CHRISTINA: But they have to do what they're told. They're mums.

SUSAN: Exactly. But we don't.

CHRISTINA: Says who?

SUSAN: When I grow up I'm gonna be famous, and I'm gonna wear what I want, eat what I want, do what I want and have men, workers, cooking and cleaning and feeding and me and no one will tell me what to do. Ever.

CHRISTINA: Why won't you look at me?

SUSAN: Because my dad told me not to.

CHRISTINA: Why not?

SUSAN: He said I have to avoid anything mildly entertaining.

CHRISTINA: We can't not look at each other ever again.

SUSAN: He said it's the only way to control the laughing. I don't want to make you laugh.

CHRISTINA: Why would you make me laugh. You aren't even funny.

SUSAN: It's not me. It's because you have a funny face.

(*She giggles. They hold their breath. It passes.*)

CHRISTINA: Do I really have a funny face?

SUSAN: No, you're pretty.

CHRISTINA: Eric doesn't think it's pretty. He said I look like a walrus and that means he thinks I'm ugly, because walruses are disgusting.

SUSAN: He's an idiot.

CHRISTINA: No, he's not. Don't be jealous.

SUSAN: In English class he asked me how to spell orange.

(*They laugh. They hold their breath. It passes.*)

CHRISTINA: Do you think we're possessed? Because Glory said she saw the devil in the mirror of the first-floor toilets and I swear I saw Martha's eyes flash red during Maths.

SUSAN: Maybe I don't believe in God.

CHRISTINA: Maybe you're possessed because you don't believe in him? So he's punishing you?

SUSAN: That doesn't make any sense.

CHRISTINA: Your face doesn't make any sense.

(*They giggle. They hold their breath. It passes.*)

CHRISTINA: If it's not the devil, or God, then what is it?

SUSAN: I don't know. Sometimes I think maybe, it's because the world... doesn't like us.

(*They are quiet.*)

I'm sorry I gave it you.

CHRISTINA: You didn't give it to me.

SUSAN: I did.

CHRISTINA: No you didn't, okay?

SUSAN: Why are you so sure?

CHRISTINA: I just know, alright?

SUSAN: How do you know?

(*Christina is silent.*)

SUSAN: Tell me or I'll tell Eric you like him.

CHRISTINA: Fine. But don't get mad, yeah?

SUSAN: What is it?

CHRISTINA: I pretended. I was pretending that I got it too. I lied. I'm a liar and now I'm being punished for it.

SUSAN: Why would you do that?

CHRISTINA: I didn't want you to be alone. But now I'm not pretending any more and I'm scared.

SUSAN: I'm not scared. I'm just tired.

CHRISTINA: Of what?

SUSAN: Of living in a world that's not mine.

(*They are quiet for a second.*)

Let's practise for choir.

CHRISTINA: Do we have to?

SUSAN: My Dad said if we don't practise every day we could lose our voices. Forever.

(*They giggle. They forget to hold their breath. They hold hands. They sing 'Good Times' by The Persuasions in perfect harmony.*)

Scene 11

Frankenstein

Mary Shelley, adapted by LAMDA

*Victor is a scientist who creates Creature. Horrified by Creature's appearance,
Victor runs away, leaving Creature abandoned. Prior to this scene, Creature
seeks kindness from humans but is repeatedly rejected and shunned from
society. Spurred on by rage, Creature murders Victor's brother William. In this
scene, Victor and Creature meet again on a Mountain.*

(*Victor sits at the top of the Mountain. He sees a figure approaching.*)

VICTOR: Monster! Abhorred fiend! Do you dare approach me?

CREATURE: I expected this reception.

VICTOR: Begone, vile insect! Or rather, stay, that I may trample you to dust.

CREATURE: You purpose to kill me?

VICTOR: Yes, and I will –

(*Victor, enraged, prepares to attack Creature.*)

CREATURE: Remember, Frankenstein, thou hast made me more powerful than
thyself. My height is superior to thine, my joints more supple.

VICTOR: Then let us try our strength in a fight, in which one must fall.

CREATURE: I will not be tempted to set myself in opposition to thee.

VICTOR: We are enemies.

CREATURE: *I* am thy creature. I ought to be thy Adam!

VICTOR: How do you...?

CREATURE: *Paradise Lost.*

VICTOR: You've read *Paradise Lost*?

CREATURE: I liked it.

(*Beat.*)

CREATURE: Frankenstein: I entreat you to hear me.

VICTOR: I will not.

CREATURE: Adam had his Creator, but where was mine?

VICTOR: I curse my own hands for forming you. You – a murderer!

CREATURE: You accuse me of murder; and yet you would, with a satisfied conscience, destroy your own creature. I ask you not to spare me: listen to me; and then, if you can, and if you will, destroy the work of your hands.

VICTOR: I will not hear you. Begone!

CREATURE: Believe me, Frankenstein: I was benevolent; my soul glowed with love and humanity: but am I not alone, miserably alone? You, my creator, abhor me; what hope can I gather from your fellow creatures, who owe me nothing? They spurn and hate me. But on you it rests whether I lead a harmless life or become the author of your own speedy ruin. We will not part until you have promised to comply with my requisition.

VICTOR: What would have me do?

CREATURE: No one will associate with me; but one as deformed and horrible as myself –

VICTOR: What?

CREATURE: She would not deny herself to me.

VICTOR: She?

CREATURE: I want a companion. This being you must create.

(*Victor is stunned.*)

VICTOR: I refuse it.

CREATURE: You alone can do this.

VICTOR: Create another like yourself?

CREATURE: If you do not, I will desolate your heart.

VICTOR: You shall never make me base in my own eyes. Shall I create another like yourself, whose joint wickedness might desolate the world?

CREATURE: What I ask of you is reasonable and moderate –

VICTOR: I have answered you; you may torture me, but I will never consent.

CREATURE: We shall be monsters, cut off from the world.

VICTOR: No – you will return, and your evil passions will be renewed, and you will then have a companion to aid you. This may not be.

CREATURE: I swear to you, by the earth which I inhabit, and by you that made me, that, with the companion you bestow, I will dwell in the most savage of places. My life will flow quietly away, and, in my dying moments, I shall not curse my maker.

(*Beat.*)

(*Creature's words have an impact on Victor.*)

VICTOR: You propose to fly from the habitations of humankind, to dwell in those wilds where the beasts of the field will be your only companions?

CREATURE: Neither you nor any other human being shall ever see us again.

VICTOR: You swear to be harmless?

CREATURE: The love of another will destroy the cause of my crimes, and I shall become a thing of whose existence everyone will be ignorant.

(*Long pause.*)

VICTOR: I consent to your demand, on your solemn oath to quit Europe for ever.

CREATURE: I swear that you shall never behold me again.

(*Creature leaves, descending the mountain.*)

Chapter 10

Level 2 Acting: Grade 5 Solo

Wonder Boy

Ross Willis

*Roshi is cast as Hamlet in the school production of 'Hamlet'. In this speech,
Roshi describes the plot of Hamlet to their friend Sonny, who is playing one of
the Guards.*

*(The lockers. After school. Sonny runs in.
Roshi jumps out from a locker terrifying him.
Roshi is holding a skull.
Dressed in FULL-ON ye olde Shakespearean gear.)*

ROSHI: HAMLET'S BASICALLY A BAD VERSION OF THE LION KING.
THERE'S THIS BLOKE CALLED HAMLET
HE'S LIKE IF SIMBA WAS TOTALLY BASIC
SO THERE ARE THESE TWO GUARDS
ONE OF THEM YOUS!!!!!
THEY'RE OUSTIDE FREEZIN AND THEY SEE A GHOST OF HAMLET'S DEAD
DAD AND THEY'RE LIKE OHMYGOD THAT'S SO RANDOM WE SHOULD
TELL HAMLET.
MEANWHILE, HAMLET'S DAD JUST DIED AND HIS MUM GOT REMARRIED
TO HAMLET'S UNCLE SUPER-QUICK.
HE'S GOT THAT FEELIN WHEN YOUS GO TO THE MALL AND SEE
CHRISTMAS DECORATIONS THE DAY AFTER HALLOWEEN.
HAMLET'S MUM IS LIKE A HUMAN PROP WHO DOES NOTHIN.
LIKE SHAKEY P JUST WHEELS HER OUT BUT SHE DOESN'T REALLY DO
ANYTHIN.
SHE'S A PERSONALITY VACUUM.
SO HAMLET'S DEAD DAD COMES UP TO HAMLET AND IS LIKE
YO YOUR UNCLE MURDERED ME I WAS HAVING A NAP AND HE'S ALL LIKE
TAKE SOME EAR POISON
HAMLET IS LIKE SHOCKED PIKACHU FACE.
HAMLET'S DEAD DAD IS LIKE LOL YEAH YOUS SHOULD PROBABLY KILL HIM.
BUT I'M LIKE HMMM HOLD ON
WHY HAS THE GHOST WAITED NEARLY A MONTH SINCE THE MARRIAGE
BEFORE SHOWIN ITSELF?
BUT HAMLET'S DEAD DAD IS LIKE GOTTAGOBYE AND THEN FOR LIKE
MOST OF THE PLAY HAMLET PROCRASTINATES
HAMLET GETS DEPRESSED BECAUSE HE ISN'T AS COOL AS SIMBA.
HAMLET'S EVIL UNCLE DOESN'T EVEN SING 'BE PREPARED' SO HE CAN
GO AWAY
HAMLET WAS SEEIN THIS GIRL OPHELIA
ANOTHER HUMAN PROP

HE'D SLIDE INTO HIS DM 'U UP BABE'
OPHELIA IS LIKE 'YEAHS' LIKE
HAMLET IS LIKE 'HERE'S A CAT PICTURE'
OPHELIA IS LIKE 'OHMYGOD I LOVE YOU'.
AND THEN HAMLET SETS OUT TO AVENGE HIS FATHER'S MURDER
AND GETS HIS ENTIRE FAMILY AND EVERYONE ELSE IN THE PLAY KILLED
SO BASICALLY HAMLET DECIDES TO PUT ON A SHOW AND IS ALL LIKE
WITH JAZZ HANDS I WILL MAKE MY UNCLE
CONFESS TO MURDER
BUT IT DOESN'T WORK
AND HAMLET IS REALLY LIKE SURE IT NEARLY WORKED CUZ HIS UNCLE
FARTS OR SOMETHIN THEN HE ACCIDENTALLY KILLS OPHELIA'S DAD
BECAUSE HE HATES THE CURTAINS IN THE ROOM.
AND THEN OPHELIA FALLS IN A PUDDLE AND DROWNS AND EVERYONE'S
LIKE WHATEVER AND HAMLET GOES TO HER FUNERAL LIKE FEEL LIKE
SHIT JUST WANT HER BACK.
POUNDLAND TIMON AND PUMBAA DIE AND LIKE NO ONE CARES
HAMLET GETS CASUALLY KIDNAPPED BY PIRATES JUST CUZ...
AND THEN HAMLET'S MUM IS ALL LIKE
LOL I'M THIRSTY AND DRINKS SOME POISON
AND EVERYONE'S LIKE WHATEVER
AND HAMLET FINALLY KILLS HIS UNCLE.
AND HAMLET KILLS LAERTES.
AND LAERTES KILLS HAMLET.
AND ALL OF THIS COULD HAVE BEEN STOPPED
IF
AT
ANY
POINT
SOMEONE

ANYONE

TOLD HAMLET TO

SHUT

UP!!!!!!!!

Scene 8

Listen To Your Parents

Benjamin Zephaniah

---

*The Campbells are a Black British family living in Birmingham. Mark Campbell
is pursuing his dreams of becoming a footballer and poet. Yet as he does so,
his family life becomes increasingly troubled through violent outbursts from his
father. In this speech, he talks about his dreams for the future, and vows that he
will never follow his father's violence.*

MARK: (*Shouts.*) Go forth and score. (*Speaking quickly – excited as he shows
off his books.*) Yes. Wicked. Check this out, this one's poetry, and this one's
football. This one's called 'Oh My Word' and it's lots of short poems and raps by
different poets. Fun poems you know, word play and stuff like that. And this one,
well it's easy ain't it? 'The Complete Encyclopaedia of Aston Villa'. Brilliant or
what? I said I would do it and now this is serious, I'm gonna start me own little
library. Mom said if I look after these I could get more when she can afford it.
Not bad hey? And I wasn't even expecting anything.

This is what happened right. We were coming from school, Mom was doing
her shopping, Carlton was in his pushchair, Angela was there, talking, talking,
talking. Then we stopped to buy some vegetables and then after that I saw
right in front of me, in the window of a bookshop, this book, the poetry one.
Because I got it from the library before I knew it was really funny so I said to me
Mom that one day I'll get me own copy of that. Then we went into the bookshop
and we started just looking around and Mom saw this book she liked about
Jamaica, and then I saw this big Villa book. So I started looking at the pictures
and me Mom came up to me and said do I really want a book to take home, and
I said yes, and she said which one and I said, 'Boy it's so hard to choose.' Then
she went away, in a corner like, and I saw her looking in her purse and counting
all her money and then, guess what? She came back and said I could have
both, I couldn't believe it guy, both of them. And then guess what? She bought
a book about horses for Angela, and she bought that book about Jamaica for
herself. Look at that man, I can't believe it, brand new, don't mess, and I don't
even have to take it back to the library.

(*Beat.*)

You wait, it's gonna happen, guy. One day you'll see me in the paper, Mark
Anthony Campbell, footballer and poet, so watch out. I ain't showing off or
anything, I just know what I know. Me poems are gonna make people laugh and

cry, they're gonna be like intelligent poems that make people think about things going on in the world. And maybe I'll get meself a big house like Aston Hall, you know those types of houses that have a long drive and a garden like a park, that kind of house. And if I get married, I might marry a poet, yes guy, a poet wife for a poet husband... I wonder if Maria Shah is really a poet. Anyway check this out, I had this idea right, we could even have a poet priest to marry us, so he could say something like:

'Do you take this poet as your lawful wedded wife?
Do you want to live with her for all your life?
She's cool and she's wicked and she's standing at your side,
So do it poet, drop a rhyme and kiss your lovely bride.'

(*Slowing down the pace.*) But I tell you what, I wouldn't hit her. I wouldn't marry someone and then beat them up, what's that for? Why marry someone and then spend so much time beating them up? If I really get upset and lose me temper, I'll just go for a walk or write a poem. I'd just say, 'We must talk dis ting over Maria,' and then we would talk about it, you know what I mean? If Angela had a husband and he hit her I would fight him but that's different ain't it? That's helping Angela, defending me sister but I ain't gonna be no wife-beater.

Scene 13, 'Friday'

Votes for Women

Elizabeth Robins, adapted by LAMDA

Vida is a suffragette living in London, preparing to lead a rally in Trafalgar Square. This speech is her public address to the crowd in Trafalgar Square, where she advocates for women's rights.

(*Vida comes to the edge of the platform.*)

VIDA: You've seen the accounts of the girl who's been tried in Manchester lately for the murder of her child. Not pleasant reading. Even if we'd noticed it, we wouldn't speak of it in my world. A few months ago I should have turned away my eyes and forgotten even the headline as quickly as I could. But since that morning in the police-court, I read these things. This, as you'll remember, was about a little working girl – an orphan of eighteen – who crawled with the dead body of her new-born child to her master's back-door, and left the baby there. She dragged herself a little way off and fainted. A few days later she found herself in court, being tried for the murder of her child. Her master – a married man – had of course reported the 'find' at his back-door to the police, and he had been summoned to give evidence. The girl cried out to him in the open court, 'You are the father!' He couldn't deny it. The Coroner at the jury's request censured the man, and regretted that the law didn't make him responsible. But he went scot-free. And that girl is now serving her sentence in Strangeways Gaol.

A woman is arrested by a man, brought before a man judge, tried by a jury of men, condemned by men, taken to prison by a man, and by a man she's hanged! Where in all this were her 'peers'? Why did men so long ago insist on trial by 'a jury of their peers'? So that justice shouldn't miscarry – wasn't it? A man's peers would best understand his circumstances, his temptation, the degree of his guilt. Yet there's no such unlikeness between different classes of men as exists between man and woman. What man has the knowledge that makes him a fit judge of woman's deeds at that time of anguish – that hour – (*Lowers her voice and bends over the crowd.*) – that hour that some woman struggled through to put each man here into the world. I noticed when a previous speaker quoted the Labour Party you applauded. Some of you here – I gather – call yourselves Labour men. Every woman who has borne a child is a Labour woman. No man among you can judge what she goes through in her hour of darkness – (*Catching her fluttering breath, goes on very low.*) - in that great agony when, even under the best conditions that money and devotion can buy, many a woman falls into temporary mania, and not a few go down to death.

In the case of this poor little abandoned working girl, what man can be the fit judge of her deeds in that awful moment of half-crazed temptation? Women know of these things as those know burning who have walked through fire.

(*Vida leans over the platform and speaks with a low and thrilling earnestness.*)

I would say in conclusion to the women here, it's not enough to be sorry for these our unfortunate sisters. We must get the conditions of life made fairer. We women must organise. We must learn to work together. We have all (rich and poor, happy and unhappy.) worked so long and so exclusively for men, we hardly know how to work for one another. But we must learn.

Act 2, 'Trafalgar Square, London'

My Son's a Queer (But What Can You Do?)

Rob Madge

Madge is a queer, non-binary person growing up in Birmingham. At the age of twelve, they decide to put on a Disney Parade for their Grandma, involving Ariel, Belle, missed cues and faulty props. In this speech, Madge outlines Step Two of their plan for the Parade: finding the right costume.

MADGE: Step Two. If you want to help your children put on a parade, find the costume that works for you. After years of fashioning my Dad's Oakland A's top into Peter Pan's tunic or Winifred Sanderson's dress I figure it's time for an upgrade and I finally get my first proper costume in a tale as old as time... It's 2002. Dad's just got back from a work trip. He carries a Disney store bag. I race over to it. 'Please be the Belle dress, please be the Belle dress'. (*Sees that it is not, in fact, the Belle dress.*) 'Knew you always wanted the Beast outfit'. Once I get over my initial disappointment, I put on that Beast's head and it's in that moment that we reach, in the words of Sarah Brightman, the point of no return. 'Attention parents. Let it be known that I will stop at nothing till I have every prop, every costume, every smoke machine from here to Sandwell and Dudley'. And just like that, our little house in the Midlands slowly begins to transform into the wardrobe department of the London Palladium. It gets to the point where Dad has to google storage units for the expansion of the fancy-dress box. But when we go shopping, there's nothing about the Princes or the Spidermen or the Beasts that spark my interest. What I really want is that yellow Belle dress. Only problem is, that's in the girls' section of the shop. 'I d'ay think Mommy'll be too pleased you coming home in that'. (*Now, themself as a child, butching up.*) 'So sorry. Thought it was Buzz Lightyear. Sorry. Long day of fractions. Dizzy playing Heads Down, Thumbs Up. So sorry. My mistake.'

(*The sound of jingle bells.*)

Christmas time. I'm at a local amdram panto when I see, out of the heavens, descending from a rickety, rhine-stoned moon... Maleficent. I am bewitched. She's bedazzled in this dark purple, huge-collared gown and these horns that, in my eyes, go up to the gods. I look up the actress' name... Tim. I know what I need to do then. I need to be Maleficent. She could be played by anyone. Angelina Jolie, Tim. She won't be in the girls' section. She'll be in the Anybody Brilliant and Powerful section. Turns out there is no section. It's just the same old two options. (*Spies a suitcase.*) But I do have a Brilliant and Powerful Grandmother. My Grandma, or Granny Grimble as she's known on Equity... 'Grandma' was already taken... she's always hard at work behind the scenes.

Knitting and sewing and making me lederhosen out of curtains for my revival of *The Sound of Music* in the garage. So, when I decide I need to be Maleficent, I phone Granny Grimble as I always do at do at 6.30pm, just after *The Weakest Link* (anything before 6 costs to ring on the landline) and I tell her it's time. It's time to play the part I've always wanted to play.

(*With a delicate flourish, Madge reveals a homemade Maleficent dress from the suitcase, sewn by Granny Grimble. Beat. Madge turns to us.*)

So find the costume that works for you. And if you can't, phone your Grandma after *The Weakest Link*. She'll sort you out.

De Monfort
Joanna Baillie

Ever since childhood, De Monfort has despised his schoolmate Rezenvelt, when they encountered each other in a duel that Rezenvelt won. When the pair cross paths again, De Monfort's hatred grows into pure rage. In this speech, De Monfort hides the forest, awaiting Rezenvelt's arrival and the opportunity to take his revenge.

(Moonlight. A wild path in a wood, shaded with trees. Enter De Monfort, with a strong expression of disquiet, mixed with fear, upon his face, looking behind him, and bending his ear to the ground, as if he listened to something.)

DE MONFORT: How hollow groans the earth beneath my tread!
Is there an echo here? Methinks it sounds
As tho' some heavy footstep follow'd me.
I will advance no father.
Deep settled shadows rest across the path,
And thickly-tangled boughs o'erhang this spot.
O that a tenfold gloom did cover it!
That 'midst the murky darkness I might strike;
As in the wild confusion of a dream,
Thinks horrid, bloody, terrible do pass,
As tho' they pass'd not; nor impress the mind
With the fix'd clearness of reality.

(An owl is heard screaming near him.)

(Starting.) What sound is that?

(Listens, and the owl cries again.)

It is the screech-owl's cry.
Foul bird of night! what spirit guides thee here?
Art thou instinctive drawn to scenes of horror?
I've heard of this.

(Pauses and listens.)

How those fall'n leaves so rustle upon the path,
With whisp'ring noise, as tho' the earth around me

Did utter secret things!
The distant river too, bears to mine ear
A dismal wailing. O mysterious night!
Thou art not silent; many tongues hast thou.
A distant gath'ring blast sounds thro' the wood,
And dark clouds fleetly hasten o'er the sky:
O! that a storm would rise, a raging storm;
Amidst the roar of warring elements
I'd lift my hand and strike! but this pale light,
This calm distinctness of each silly thing,
Is terrible. (*Starting.*) Footsteps are near –
He comes! he comes! I'll watch him father on –
I cannot do it here.

Act 4, Scene 3

The Diary of a Hounslow Girl

Ambreen Razia

Shaheeda is a sixteen-year-old British Muslim girl grappling with growing up, traditional values, friendship and relationships. Shaheeda enters a relationship with a boy named Aaron, but he starts to ignore her. Noticing a change in Shaheeda's behaviour, her sister Aisha asks if she is okay. This speech is Shaheeda's reaction.

SHAHEEDA: I looked at her, ready to tell her everything, about how I fell in love and lost my two best friends, didn't do my GCSEs, discovered things about myself that I never really knew, like my love for poetry, and that I'm gonna be a mum… at sixteen, and that I wished I could have been like you and could have done everything by the book but there's something either very wrong or very right with me and I can't work it out because I haven't had time because… Because… (*She pauses, catches her breath and exhales.*) And before I had a chance to speak I felt my mum grab me by the arm and say: '*Kya hogya tomhe? Abka shakel itna harab he!*' If you can't be happy Shaheeda, then go home.

I wasn't going to cry. Not in front of all these people and just as I felt my chest tightening and the tears coming, I legged it. I left the Valima, I ran through Beaverfield Park, down Heathdale Avenue, and I could see the Integration Centre getting further and further away as I looked back, disappearing into the distance and people were looking at me like I was crazy, running through Hounslow with my salwar kameez, like I was running away from my own wedding or something. (*Beat.*) I ran so fast that I got to Aaron's house in the space of ten minutes. I wasn't even sure about what I was there to say, or what he was gonna say when he saw me in the state I was in. I rung his doorbell and there was no answer but his window was wide open and he always closed it when he went out so I thought he must just be blanking me like he had been doing for the past six weeks when I needed him the most and I couldn't work out why, I mean I didn't know what I had done to mess this all up? Aaron?

(*She looks up at a window.*)

I've tried to ring you, but your phone's off. I just wanted to let you know that I'm ready. Packed! And I know you've seen all my messages this month coz I can see the double blue ticks on all the *WhatsApps* I've sent.

(She looks around her as if she is standing outside his window and people are walking past.)

Look. This thing I need to chat to you about, it's important. Like proper important. Like World War Three important... (*Pause, she waits for a response.*) I saw Miss Middleton at Hounslow East, she stopped me and said that I'll have to retake my GCSEs next year with Sinead O'Brian and Lacy Adams. She said that I had a lot of potential, you know? Her exact words were that I have 'a natural ability to retain information and I just get things quicker and that if I had put it to good use I'd be a proper success.' And do you know what I said? Aaron, do you know what I said?

I said that I remember what Aaron was wearing when I first saw him. I could tell you every single tattoo he has and what they all mean. I remember our first kiss like it was yesterday and how both his eyebrows rise when he's waiting for an answer to a question. I told her not to worry and that my ability to retain important information had been put to good use.

(Pause.)

Aaron?

Part 3, Scene 1, 'The Valima'

Hamish

Jack Thorne

It is 1981 and the electric wheelchair is available to purchase, but not yet available on the NHS. Hamish's parents organise a fundraiser to buy Hamish a new, self-operated wheelchair. In this speech, Hamish recounts his experience of using an electric wheelchair for the first time.

Recommended reading age for the full script is 15+.

HAMISH: They'd done a radging meat raffle, done a stall at the fair, I saw my poor old da standing in front of the tombola. Jar on the bar for change. Charity singalongs. Non-school-uniform day at the school where ma waves a lollipop. They'd sold themselves again and again, trying to get the money together.

And it had come. Eight hundred and eight-five pounds of it, plus ten pounds delivery.

My ma had this grin on her face as the truck came down the road. Neighbours standing in the road. Alan, Deirdre, Blythe, Mark and bawbag Derek. International Year of Disability and they'd given two pounds to make themselves feel a little bit less bad.

There it is – the BEC-14 with speed control and direct rear-wheel drive.

I'm loading in and to whooping and applause I'm soon whizzing up and down the street.

'How does it handle, Hamish?' 'Handles great, Da.' More clapping.

But people are bored and turning away even as they do. That's enough with the lad in the chair. He's had his moment. We've had our two pounds' worth.

Then it's time for tea. Da goes back to his girlfriend's, me and Ma linger, as is our way, and wash ready for bed. But no way am I doing that.

I've always needed someone to push me wherever I needed to go.

I've always felt someone's breath on the back of my neck. Not tonight. I wait forty minutes, quiet as a mouse, takes some doing but then I'm out and I'm free.

You don't get freedom like this on the NHS – the meat raffles have paid – and I am free. On the BEC-14.

Four miles an hour, midnight, wind in my hair, pass the house of Alan, Deirdre, Blythe, Mark and bawbag Derek. I've known them all, all my life. With their sorrowful looks towards my mother. I pass Mrs McGoonagh weaving down the street in her mini-skirt. 'Hello, pet,' I say.

She looks astonished. I know she'll tell my ma as soon as she sobers up. I don't care. Six miles per hour.

Ridgemount Hill. The wheels are screaming. I'm screaming.

YEEEEEAAAAAAHHHHHHH!!!!!

AAAAAAAAAAAHHHHHHHHHH!

And there it is – laid out in front of me – Cratchit Woods.

Women of Troy

Euripides, translated by **Kenneth McLeish**

In Troy, the city is torn apart by the Greeks. Soldiers die and the Women of Troy remain. Cassandra, the daughter of Priam and Hecuba, can see the future. She knows that she is destined to become Agamemnon's wife. Speaking to her mother, Cassandra weaponises her future marriage.

(*No man's land, between the shattered walls of Troy and the tents of the victorious Greeks. Night. Enter Cassandra with torches.*)

CASSANDRA: Rejoice, mother.
Crown me with flowers. I've won.
I'm marrying a king. Take me to him;
Make me, give me no choice.
Trust Apollo. If God is god,
This marriage will ruin His Lordship.
Agamemnon, grand admiral of Greece!
I'll hurt him more than Helen did.
I'll kill him, strip all his house
Till the price is paid
For my father and brothers dead.
Cassandra, hush! Don't tell it all:
Don't sing of knives, necks chopped,
Mine and those others',
Blood-feud, the mother dead,
The dynasty destroyed.
My marriage-price!
Sane now, no madness,
I tell you this: God's words.
We outrank the Greeks. We win.
What did they do?
For one woman's sake,
They hunted Helen,
Squandered a million lives.
Agamemnon –
So experienced, so worldly-wise –
Killed what he loved for what he hated,
Threw away happiness, children, home,
For his brother's woman,
The wife who left

Of her own free choice,
Whom no one forced.
So they flocked to the Scamander,
Lined up to die
On a foreign river's banks,
On a foreign plain –
For what? Their city?
The towers of their native land?
Plucked, they'll never see
Their children; their wives' soft hands
Won't sheet them for burial.
They sleep in foreign soil.
And what of those at home?
Widows, fathers stripped of their sons,
They die alone. Who weeps for them?
Whose offerings drench their tombs?

Now, what of Troy?
What of our Trojans, dead
For their native land?
What more could they ask?
Spears snatched them. Loving hands,
Friends' hands, carried them home,
Made them decent for burial.
The earth of Troy enfolds them.
Others escaped, day after day escaped,
To smile on their wives, their children.
What Greek had that?
Is it Hector you weep for,
His cruel death? I tell you, no other man
Ever died so rich in reputation –
And that was the gift of Greeks.
If they'd stayed at home,
Who now would know his name?
And Paris. He could have married
A nobody, a name on no one's lips.
Instead: Helen of Sparta,
Daughter of Zeus on high.
If wars must be fought,

A glorious death, not a coward's,
Brings honour to the city.
You see? Mother? Don't weep for Troy.
Don't weep for me.
Your enemies, my enemies –
I'll marry, and destroy them all.

Candida

George Bernard Shaw, adapted by LAMDA

Marchbanks is a strange, shy poet who is in love with Candida, the wife of Reverend Morell. Candida is fifteen years his senior, but Marchbanks firmly believes that his love is reciprocated. In this speech, Marchbanks decides to challenge Morell's marriage.

MARCHBANKS: I must speak to you. There is something that must be settled between us. (*Passionately.*) Now. Before you leave this room.

(*He retreats a few steps, and stands as if to bar Morell's way to the door.*)

Don't look at me in that self-complacent way. You think yourself stronger than I am; but I shall stagger you if you have a heart in your breast.

First –

I love your wife.

(*Morell recoils, and, after staring at him for a moment in utter amazement, bursts into uncontrollable laughter. Marchbanks is taken aback, but not disconcerted; and he soon becomes indignant and contemptuous.*)

Do you think that the things people make fools of themselves about are any less real and true than the things they behave sensibly about? (*Morell's gaze wavers.*) They are more true: they are the only things that are true. You are very calm and sensible and moderate with me because you can see that I am a fool about your wife; just as no doubt that old man who was here just now is very wise over your socialism, because he sees that YOU are a fool about it. (*Morell's perplexity deepens markedly. Marchbanks follows up his advantage, plying him fiercely with questions.*) Does that prove you wrong? Does your complacent superiority to me prove that I am wrong? I told you I should stagger you.

(*Morell advances on him threateningly.*)

(*Shrinking back.*) Let me alone. Don't touch me. Stop, Morell. I won't bear it. (*Almost in hysterics.*) I'm not afraid of you: it's you who are afraid of me. You think because I shrink from being brutally handled – because (*With tears in his voice.*) I can do nothing but cry with rage when I am met with violence –

because I can't lift a heavy trunk down from the top of a cab like you – because I can't fight you for your wife as a navvy would: all that makes you think that I'm afraid of you. But you're wrong.

(*Morell, angered, turns on him again. Marchbanks flies to the door in involuntary dread.*)

Let me alone, I say. I'm going. Tell her what I said. If you don't tell her, I will: I'll write to her. She will understand me, and know that I understand her.

Act 1

Offside
Sabrina Mahfouz and **Hollie McNish**

Lily Parr was a real person from Lancashire who lived in the 1900s, playing football during the First World War for Dick Kerr's Ladies, a factory team. She was the first woman in the football hall of fame. In this speech, it is 1921 and teenage Lily is playing football, but she's up against obstacles. The Football Association are trying to ban women from playing the game. Despite this, Lily's commitment does not waver.

LILY: I played it with my heart and soul
I did.
Left foot to lamppost and back again.
Ten years of my life spent kicking a ball,
most of them hidden away down alleyways.
War-time made it our time,
time to take a ball to a field as big as the sky
not just stuck down an alley –
left foot to lamppost and back again.
Left foot to lamppost and back again.
At the factory,
some said we'd not have enough players for a team.
But we did.
Said we'd not get any matches. But we did.
Said no one would want to watch. But they did.
Said no one would keep watching.
But they did.
They just kept buying tickets,
punters turning turnstiles clicking across the country
from Preston to Glasgow,
London to Liverpool.
But the men are back from war
and they – meaning the FA,
don't want us playing this *'man's game'* anymore.
In one match we had 53,000 spectators last year,
now they ban us from the grounds saying
you're not welcome here?
This match we played last week was a final protest,
representing all women's teams in the country,
to try and stop the whistles blowing *stop* on our dreams...

My eyes were on the ball, they always are.
My eyes and my left foot,
cos of them I scored forty-three goals in my first season alone,
coming up to about four hundred all in all now.
I ran quick like I used to do as a kid in the back streets
off to find blackberries for the jam we lived off,
but my focus was off –
I knew those FA fools were in the crowd.
Tens of thousands of people
but I just wanted to see *their* faces, *their* eyes.
Catch them, keep them on me
as I speed down the pitch they want to ban me from
just because I'm a flipping woman.
I've scored more goals than they've ever seen!
I stumbled, felt the taste of mud in my mouth,
swore – sorry Mum – as I spat it out.
The other team scored, but so what,
I just cared that those 'officials' could sit there now and say
see, she can't even keep herself off the ground –

I got up.
I always get up.
I was running towards the net
about to kick the ball,
another goal to get,
I've got the most of any girl,
when I froze.
In the seat in front of me, where my dad always sat,
there they were, those red faces I'd been searching for,
the FA officials, taking up the space my dad should be at,
now he was a few rows back.
These matches we've been playing for four years
have made more money for our lads back from war
than the bloody government or the FA ever has –
posh puckered lips sipping sweet tea in the capital
and my anger is tangible, I won't slip up again,
I kick that ball so hard my toe cracks –
back of the net, how d'ya like that!

Scene 2

Level 2 Acting: Grade 5 Duologue

Noughts & Crosses

Sabrina Mahfouz, adapted from the novel by **Malorie Blackman**

Sephy is a Cross, and the daughter of the Home Secretary. Callum is a Nought. The Noughts and Crosses are separated through racial and social divides; therefore, Sephy and Callum's teenage friendship and growing romance is forbidden. In this scene, Sephy is being held to ransom by the Liberation Militia (LM), where Callum serves.

(Sephy wraps a bandage around her finger. Callum starts watching for a bit, about to say something, then turns to go.)

SEPHY: They've gone then?

CALLUM: Yeah.

SEPHY: I'm quite flattered that one of me could be worth five whole LM members. I guess that's the value system us Crosses have set out, so in a way, you're playing by our rules, even when you're breaking them all.

CALLUM: You should drink something.

(Sephy picks up the bottle and regards it, smiles at Callum and he half-smiles back. Then her whole face changes and she throws it at the wall.)

SEPHY: What's the point when you're going to kill me?!

CALLUM: Sephy, what are you doing?

SEPHY: None of you are wearing masks, I could identify you all. Even if Father does everything you lot want, I'm still going to die.

CALLUM: That's not the deal.

SEPHY: Callum, don't be so naive.

CALLUM: We're setting the terms of the deal and we'll keep them. We'll show you how we treat power with respect.

SEPHY: How can something be respectful when it's been gained like this?

CALLUM: So Crosses gained their power respectfully, did they? With tea and cake and no bloodshed?

SEPHY: That's not what I'm saying. I know it was obtained in ways that should make every Cross ashamed. But that does not mean condoning actions of equivalent violence, aggression and evil from Noughts, this won't solve anything!

CALLUM: So you've read a couple of books now, have you?

SEPHY: I... have learnt a lot at boarding school. While you've been training to be this... soldier, I've been training myself too, you know, retraining, rather. Looking at things clearly, for the first time. Truly seeing how things have been set up by us to favour us and we have used every awful thing available to keep it this way. We have the riches, the control of resources, the opportunities, the land, the property and then it all perpetuates because we keep the status quo going and how can anyone compete?

CALLUM: Three years is a long time to be reading. What have you actually done?

SEPHY: That is what I've done. That is my action. Learning. I have to learn before I can act otherwise my actions will be wrong. I plan to dedicate my career to finding peaceful solutions to all this...

CALLUM: There's no peaceful solution except for segregation to end.

SEPHY: I got hold of books from other places where people live equally, everything shared and each individual doing whatever it is that they're skilled in, with skin colour playing no part whatsoever – imagine! We can build this, we can build it for the future, but we have to do it together –

CALLUM: Noughts have been trying to work peacefully with Crosses – Crosses like your dad, Sephy – for decades. It doesn't work. Nothing changes. And have you ever really tried – I mean really tried – to influence your father to change things?

SEPHY: There are other ways to make change: I've hosted panels, organised conferences, sit-ins and protests –

CALLUM: Crosses aren't going to give up all those years of privilege and status with a little conference and a couple of panel talks. Always a kid. Keep your bloody sit-ins, Sephy, and I'll keep my way. This is the only thing they'll truly see and hear, this.

SEPHY: Fine. Let's not talk again until you have to end my life in, oh I guess around ten hours' time. I hope it's you that kills me. I'll beg for it to be you, to stare in your eyes as you do –

CALLUM: Stop!

SEPHY: Why? You don't care, you never did.

CALLUM: I did. I... I do.

SEPHY: Then let me go. I'd never say I saw you.

CALLUM: No. I can't, Sephy. Even if I wanted to.

SEPHY: Do you at least? Want to?

CALLUM: I have to be what I have to be, Sephy, not who I was or who I might want to be.

SEPHY: That doesn't even make sense.

CALLUM: Sephy.

SEPHY: What, Callum?

(*Beat. Callum is not sure he should do this. He brings out the letter.*)

CALLUM: Did you mean this, when you wrote it?

SEPHY: You couldn't be bothered to answer it, but you managed to keep it? You're unbelievable.

CALLUM: I... I just got it. Mum never saw me, till now, she kept it. Sephy, were you really prepared to go away with me? To risk all that? You felt all that... for me?

(*Beat. All the air is sucked out of her world. He never knew.*)

SEPHY: I... was a fool. A little kid, like you said.

(*Sephy is upset.*)

Please go, Callum.

CALLUM: Let me see your finger.

(*He takes her hand and it's like a switch going on, they are completely magnetised by each other.*)

SEPHY: Are you a doctor now as well as a freedom fighter?

(*Beat.*)

It hurts –

(*Callum unwraps her clumsy bandaging and does an expert, gentle job. He is so tender and they get closer and closer until their noses are almost touching. Callum is finishing the bandaging as he says without looking up –*)

CALLUM: Sephy, I would have gone with you.

SEPHY: What?

(*He looks her in the eyes, holds her face.*)

CALLUM: I was too scared to ever say it before, but I thought it, all the time. I love you, Sephy, I always did.

Act 2

The Duchess of Malfi
John Webster, adapted by LAMDA

Ferdinand and the Cardinal are brothers of the Duchess of Malfi. In this scene, Ferdinand enters with a letter, bringing news that their sister is pregnant. Both the Cardinal and Ferdinand believe the child is illegitimate, and whilst this news sends Ferdinand into a rage, Cardinal displays calculated emotional detachment.

(*Enter Cardinal and Ferdinand with a letter.*)

FERDINAND: I have this night digg'd up a mandrake.

CARDINAL: Say you?

FERDINAND: And I am grown mad with't.

CARDINAL: What's the prodigy?

FERDINAND: Read there, a sister damn'd: she's loose I'th' hilts;
Grown a notorious strumpet.

CARDINAL: Speak lower.

FERDINAND: Lower!
Rogues do not whisper't now, but seek to publish't
(As servants do the bounty of their lords)
Aloud; and with a covetous searching eye,
To mark who note them. O, confusion seize her!
She hath had most cunning bawds to serve her turn,
And more secure conveyances for lust
Than towns of garrison for service.

CARDINAL: Is't possible?
Can this be certain?

FERDINAND: Rhubarb, O, for rhubarb
To purge this choler! Here's the cursed day
To prompt my memory; and here't shall stick
Till of her bleeding heart I make a sponge
To wipe it out.

CARDINAL: Why do you make yourself
So wild a tempest?

FERDINAND: Would I could be one,
That I might toss her palace 'bout her ears,
Root up her goodly forests, blast her meads,
And lay her general territory as waste,
As she hath done her honours.

CARDINAL: Shall our blood,
The royal blood of Arragon and Castile,
Be thus attainted?

FERDINAND: Apply desperate physic:
We must not now use balsamum, but fire,
The smarting cupping-glass, for that's the mean
To purge infected blood, such blood as hers.
There is a kind of pity in mine eye,
I'll give it to my handkerchief; and now 'tis here,
I'll bequeath this to her bastard.

CARDINAL: What to do?

FERDINAND: Why, to make soft lint for his mother's wounds,
When I have hewed her to pieces.

CARDINAL: Curs'd creature!
Unequal nature, to place women's hearts
So far upon the left side!

FERDINAND: Foolish men,
That e'er will trust their honour in a bark
Made of so slight weak bulrush as is woman,
Apt every minute to sink it!

CARDINAL: Thus Ignorance, when it hath purchas'd honour,
It cannot wield it.

FERDINAND: Methinks I see her laughing: –
Excellent hyena!

CARDINAL: How idly shows this rage, which carries you,
As men convey'd by witches through the air,
On violent whirlwinds! this intemperate noise
Fitly resembles deaf men's shrill discourse,
Who talk aloud, thinking all other men
To have their imperfection.

FERDINAND: Have not you
My palsy?

CARDINAL: Yes; but I can be angry
Without this rupture: there is not in nature
A thing that makes man so deform'd, so beastly,
As doth intemperate anger. Chide yourself.
You have divers men, who never yet express'd
Their strong desire of rest, but by unrest,
By vexing of themselves. Come, put yourself
In tune.

Act 2, Scene 5

Anita and Me

Tanika Gupta, adapted from the novel by **Meera Syal**

It is 1960 in Wolverhampton, England, where Meena and Anita are best friends. As British Indian Meena rebels against the 'good Indian girl' that her parents want her to be, she starts hanging out with the outrageously sassy fifteen-year-old Anita. In this scene, Meena and Anita confide in one another: Meena expresses her reluctance to be sent to a posh grammar school, and Anita reveals that her mother has left the family home. Yet their connection is ruined by the arrival of Sam Lowbridge, and Meena realises that her and Anita's worlds are far apart.

(*Anita is sitting/hiding in the den. She is dressed in her school uniform and is crying. Meena approaches gingerly.*)

MEENA: What's up?

ANITA: Nothing.

MEENA: I'm thinking of running away.

ANITA: You daft cow. What for?

MEENA: Family want me to go to the grammar school.

ANITA: No?!

MEENA: Yeah.

ANITA: That's awful Meena. Where would you go?

MEENA: London. Head for the city lights.

ANITA: I'll come with you! Always wanted to be an actress and I've heard in London, they're desperate for actresses – all those shows and clubs and things.

MEENA: We could both be actresses!

ANITA: You got any money?

MEENA: No.

ANITA: Anywhere to stay?

MEENA: No.

ANITA: You'll starve or worse still – get murdered. London's dead dangerous if you got no mates. Best stay put and save up money so we go together.

MEENA: But grammar school?!

ANITA: Know what you mean. They're dead stuck up and weird at that school. Always got their noses up in the air and think they're better than everyone else. You'd end up looking like a horse. I love horses but I don't want me best mate to look like one.

(*Meena walks around pretending to be speak in a posh voice, her teeth sticking out.*)

MEENA: I say... I say...what – what? Toodly – pip.

(*Anita starts to laugh. Meena laughs too.*)

MEENA: 'least I stopped you from crying.

ANITA: I wasn't crying.

MEENA: Why're you wearing your school uniform in the middle of the hols? Where's Sally?

ANITA: Dunno. Waiting for her so I can ride Trixie. Got me fifth year uniform today for the new comp.

MEENA: You look bosting.

ANITA: Me mom's gone.

MEENA: Where?

ANITA: Dunno, she left a note, only Dad read it. She's gone off with a butcher from Cannock. Dad says she'll feel at home with the other scrag ends so good riddance...

MEENA: Oh Anita...

ANITA: These came this morning. She must have ordered them ages ago. She knew she was going.

(*Anita lifts her arm to show that the sleeve is hanging like a bat wing. Too big for her.*)

ANITA: And look, silly cow still hasn't a clue what my size is. I don't even know if she's ever coming back.

(*Meena stands up, leans over and hugs Anita.*)

MEENA: Sorry Nita, I really am.

(*Sam Lowbridge skulks past with a friend – Bazzer – who is a skin head. They are smoking and laughing about something. On seeing him, Anita starts flirting – flicking her hair, making eyes and smiling a lot whilst Meena looks tense.*)

MEENA: Anita!

ANITA: Don't know what you've got against Sam. He's the coolest boy 'round ere for miles. Yow got no taste.

(*Meena looks confused.*)

MEENA: But the things he says... 'bout foreigners and stuff... it's disgusting.

ANITA: Don't care about all that. All I know is I fancy the pants off Sam Lowbridge and I'm gonna get him.

MEENA: But what about me?

ANITA: What about yow? I don't wanna go out with yow do I?

MEENA: But we'd still be mates if yow 'get' Sam?

(*Anita thinks about it for a minute.*)

ANITA: Not if yow go to that posh school. Yow wouldn't want to hang with the likes of me. And I'd be dead embarrassed to be seen with a snobby, poncey grammar school chick.

MEENA: I wouldn't change. I'd still be the same me.

ANITA: Would yow still get me sweets?

MEENA: Yeah!

ANITA: We'll see then shall we?

(*As Anita walks away, Meena looks worried.*)

MEENA: See ya later 'Nita.

Act 2, Scene 2

Twelfth Night
William Shakespeare

When Viola is shipwrecked on the coast of Illyria, she disguises herself as a boy named Cesario and enters the service of Duke Orsino, who she is secretly in love with. Duke Orsino is in love with Olivia, and in this scene, he sends Cesario to woo Olivia on his behalf.

OLIVIA: Where lies your text?

VIOLA: In Orsino's bosom.

OLIVIA: In his bosom? In what chapter of his bosom?

VIOLA: To answer by the method, in the first of his heart.

OLIVIA: O, I have read it: it is heresy. Have you no more to say?

VIOLA: Good madam, let me see your face.

OLIVIA: Have you any commission from your lord to negotiate with my face? You are now out of your text: but we will draw the curtain and show you the picture. (*Unveiling.*) Look you, sir, such a one I was this present. Is't not well done?

VIOLA: Excellently done, if God did all.

OLIVIA: 'Tis in grain, sir, 'twill endure wind and weather.

VIOLA: 'Tis beauty truly blent, whose red and white
Nature's own sweet and cunning hand laid on.
Lady, you are the cruell'st she alive
If you will lead these graces to the grave
And leave the world no copy.

OLIVIA: O sir, I will not be so hard-hearted: I will give out divers schedules of my beauty. It shall be inventoried, and every particle and utensil labelled to my will. As, item, two lips indifferent red; item, two gray eyes, with lids to them; item, one neck, one chin, and so forth. Were you sent hither to praise me?

VIOLA: I see you what you are, you are too proud:
But if you were the devil, you are fair.
My lord and master loves you: O, such love
Could be but recompens'd, though you were crown'd
The nonpareil of beauty!

OLIVIA: How does he love me?

VIOLA: With adorations, fertile tears,
With groans that thunder love, with sighs of fire.

OLIVIA: Your lord does know my mind, I cannot love him.
Yet I suppose him virtuous, know him noble,
Of great estate, of fresh and stainless youth;
In voices well divulg'd, free, learn'd, and valiant,
And in dimension, and the shape of nature,
A gracious person. But yet I cannot love him:
He might have took his answer long ago.

VIOLA: If I did love you in my master's flame,
With such a suff'ring, such a deadly life,
In your denial I would find no sense,
I would not understand it.

OLIVIA: Why, what would you?

VIOLA: Make me a willow cabin at your gate,
And call upon my soul within the house;
Write loyal cantons of contemned love,
And sing them loud even in the dead of night;
Halloo your name to the reverberate hills,
And make the babbling gossip of the air
Cry out 'Olivia!' O, you should not rest
Between the elements of air and earth,
But you should pity me.

OLIVIA: You might do much.
What is your parentage?

VIOLA: Above my fortunes, yet my state is well:
I am a gentleman.

OLIVIA: Get you to your lord:
I cannot love him: let him send no more,
Unless, perchance, you come to me again,
To tell me how he takes it. Fare you well:
I thank you for your pains: spend this for me.

VIOLA: I am no fee'd post, lady; keep your purse;
My master, not myself, lacks recompense.
Love make his heart of flint that you shall love,
And let your fervour like my master's be,
Plac'd in contempt. Farewell, fair cruelty.

(*Viola exits.*)

OLIVIA: 'What is your parentage?'
'Above my fortunes, yet my state is well;
I am a gentleman.' I'll be sworn thou art:
Thy tongue, thy face, thy limbs, actions, and spirit
Do give thee five-fold blazon. Not too fast: soft! soft!
Unless the master were the man. How now?
Even so quickly may one catch the plague?
Methinks I feel this youth's perfections
With an invisible and subtle stealth
To creep in at mine eyes. Well, let it be.

Act 1, Scene 5

Red Pitch
Tyrell Williams

In present-day South London, lifelong friends Bilal (black) and Omz (black) spend their time on a football pitch named 'Red Pitch'. They dream of being professional footballers, but outside Red Pitch their home is under threat. Local shops are closing and flats are being destroyed. In this scene, Bilal is practicing his technique when Omz enters.

(Bilal is onstage by himself with his football. Bilal is pretending to be a football commentator as he does what he says.)

BILAL: ''Drop, drop' shoulder to one, 'drop, drop' shoulder to two... no, no, I don't believe it, 'drop, drop' shoulder three times. Bilal is through on goal; Bilal shoots, he scores and the crowd goes wild!! I swear you'll never see anything like this again!!!'

(Bilal celebrates his goal.)

OMZ: 'Crowd goes wild', yeah?

(Omz appears at the gate of Red Pitch, taking us out of this state and back to normal. He double-taps the cage upon entry.)

BILAL: *(Whilst 'drop, drop' shouldering.)* Come on. Them 'drop, drop' shoulders are serious!

(Omz spots Bilal's rucksack in the corner of Red Pitch.)

OMZ: You didn't take your bag to your yard?

BILAL: Na man, time wasted. I'm trying to get my work in.

(Omz pauses.)

OMZ: Bro, you live just there.

(Bilal continues practising.)

Where's Joey?

(*Bilal shoots Omz a look and then dribbles with the football.*)

BILAL: You know where Joey is.

OMZ: Relaxxx. Don't you know how to rest?

BILAL: Listen, let me educate you: anything you want in life, you're gonna have to work twice as hard to get it.

(*Omz takes the ball.*)

OMZ: Yeah, I do work twice as hard but you have to rest as well or you're gonna burn out. We've just come from a match.

BILAL: Yeah, but it was a friendly. When we make it pro, we'll be playing up to three times a week, you know.

(*Bilal takes the ball back.*)

OMZ: Yeah, I know.

BILAL: Things are gonna have to change when we go clear bruv, I'm telling you. I saw some post on Insta saying that ballers even switch up the food they eat as well.

OMZ: Not me boy. I'll be having my curry goat and rice for breakfast, rice 'n' peas with stew chicken for lunch and tuwo shinkafa and miyan taushe for dinner and still be badding it up on the pitch. (*Referencing the ball.*) Yeah.

BILAL: What do you know about tuwo shinkafa and miyan taushe?

(*Bilal passes the ball to Omz.*)

OMZ: That time your mum made some for me, Rara and my grandad init.

BILAL: Oh yeahhh. You can come back whenever you know – my mum was gassed having you lot around.

(Omz is grateful but struggles to show it. He passes the ball back to Bilal.)

Coach needs to hurry up and send us them deets for trials.

BILAL: He grew up in endz you know.

OMZ: So? He dipped time ago.

BILAL: Only 'cause his flat had mice.

OMZ: Didn't you hear coach talking crud today? Talking 'bout, how he don't wanna ever see me holding the ball for too long. My guy, if I feel like dribbling pass the whole team and scoring, I'll do it.

BILAL: Na, you don't have it in your locker.

OMZ: Look at how you're hating.

BILAL: *(Extends his arms and hands.)* Why would I hate?

OMZ: *(Mockingly, whilst extending arms and hands.)* 'Why would I hate?' That's how I know you're capping.

BILAL: There's nothing to hate on. Coach always says I remind him of a young Sancho.

OMZ: Sancho's not that sick.

BILAL: Now you're capping. On form, he's one of the hardest in the league – coach says it all the time.

OMZ: Yeah, only 'cause he used to train him up when they lived local.

BILAL: Whatever man. Imagine, Sancho came from endz and he's playing pro.

OMZ: We up next, Insha'Allah.

BILAL: Insha'Allah, most definitely.

OMZ: I used to see Sanch on the blocks, he used to come Red Pitch.

BILAL: 'Sanch' you know? He doesn't know you bro.

OMZ: Jadon Sancho came Red Pitch once you wasteman and I saw him when I was coming back from mosque. He nodded at me.

BILAL: (*Hysterical laughter.*) He don't knooow youuuuu!!

OMZ: It's mad how you're an Omz hater in disguise.

BILAL: 'Omz hater'? What do I hate on?

OMZ: You hate on me 'cause I'm a better baller.

BILAL: Better what?!

OMZ: That's why I was top goal-scorer today.

BILAL: Bro, let it go. You scored one / more goal than me.

OMZ: I scored more 'cause I'm a better footballer. Brudda, look at the goals I was scoring last season. Thirty-yarders, you could never.

BILAL: I bagged most goals last season. In the whole Sunday league.

OMZ: Ah, 'last season', 'last season', 'last season'; is that all you know?

BILAL: *You* brought it up!

OMZ: If coach let me take free kicks and pens, I would've netted more than you. I was second highest.

BILAL: I was top assists as well, you were nowhere near.

OMZ: No one cares about assists. It's about goals. Goals win you games.

BILAL: What do you have better than me?

OMZ: Everything.

BILAL: Like what?

OMZ: I'm faster than you.

BILAL: Paddiiiinnn.

OMZ: I don't know why you're making all this noise brudda.

BILAL: Aight, cool, know what...

(*Bilal goes to one end of Red Pitch, assuming the starting position taken up in 100m sprints.*)

OMZ: Get up man! I don't wanna embarrass you.

BILAL: Quick race, there and back.

OMZ: Brudda, I keep telling you man: this is Omz! You lot need to respeck it. Are you forgetting what I did when we wiped Eastside Rovers last season? When I gapped their number eight? You know donny was mad fast as well. Ahh na, the way I'll put you in a spliff and smoke you Bilz...

BILAL: Let's just race and see init.

(*Omz thinks for a second. It looks like he's walking over to join Bilal on the start line... but he goes to get the football.*)

OMZ: Like I said, I ain't tryna burn out.

Scene 2

Hedda Gabler
Henrik Ibsen, adapted by LAMDA

Hedda is married to George Tesman. Out of nowhere, Thea shows up at their door, distressed and looking for someone named Eilert Lovborg. Unbeknownst to Thea, Hedda and Eilert have history. In this scene, Hedda seeks to uncover reason of Thea's arrival and her connection with Eilert.

HEDDA: There! We have killed two birds with one stone.

THEA: What do you mean?

HEDDA: Could you not see that I wanted him to go?

THEA: Yes, to write the letter –

HEDDA: And that I might speak to you alone.

THEA: (*Confused.*) About the same thing?

HEDDA: Precisely.

THEA: But there is nothing more. Absolutely nothing!

HEDDA: Oh yes, but there is. There is a great deal more – I can see that. Sit here – and we'll have a cosy, confidential chat.

THEA: I was really on the point of going.

HEDDA: Oh, you can't be in such a hurry. Well? Now tell me something about your life at home.

THEA: Oh, that is just what I care least to speak about.

HEDDA: But to me, dear –? Why, weren't we at school together?

THEA: Yes, but you were in the class above me. And how dreadfully frightened of you I was then!

HEDDA: Afraid of me?

THEA: When we met on the stairs you always used to pull my hair.

HEDDA: Did I really?

THEA: Once you said you would burn it off my head.

HEDDA: Oh that was all nonsense, of course.

THEA: Yes, but I was so silly in those days. And since then, too – we have drifted so far – far apart from each other. Our circles have been so entirely different.

HEDDA: Well then, we must try and drift together again. Now listen. At school we called each other by our Christian names –

THEA: No, I am sure you must be mistaken.

HEDDA: No, not at all! I can remember quite distinctly. So now we are going to renew our old friendship. You must call me Hedda.

THEA: I am not used to such kindness.

HEDDA: There, there! And I shall call you my dear Thora.

THEA: My name is Thea.

HEDDA: Why, of course! I meant Thea. Now you must tell me everything – exactly as it stands.

THEA: Well, then you must question me.

HEDDA: What sort of a man is your husband, Thea? I mean – you know – in everyday life. is he kind to you?

THEA: (*Evasively.*) I am sure he means well in everything.

HEDDA: I should think he must be altogether too old for you. There is at least twenty years' difference between you, is there not?

THEA: Yes, that is true, too. We have not a thought in common – he and I.

HEDDA: But is he not fond of you? In his own way?

THEA: I don't think he cares for anyone but himself – and perhaps a little for the children.

HEDDA: And for Eilert Lovborg, Thea?

THEA: (*Looking at her.*) For Eilert Lovborg? What puts that into your head?

HEDDA: Well, my dear – I should say, when he sends you after him all the way to town. And besides, you said so yourself, to Tesman.

THEA: Did I? Yes, I suppose I did. No – I may just as well be honest. For it must all come out in any case.

HEDDA: Why, my dear Thea –?

THEA: To make a long story short: My husband did not know that I was coming.

HEDDA: What! Your husband didn't know it!

THEA: No, of course not. For that matter, he was away from home himself – he was travelling. Oh, I could bear it no longer, Hedda! I couldn't indeed – I was so utterly alone.

HEDDA: Well? And then?

THEA: So I put together some of my things – what I needed most – as quietly as possible. And then I left the house.

HEDDA: Without a word?

THEA: Yes – and took the train to town.

HEDDA: Why, my dear, good Thea – daring to do that!

THEA: What else could I possibly do?

HEDDA: But what do you think your husband will say when you go home again?

THEA: Back to him?

HEDDA: Of course.

THEA: I shall never go back to him again.

HEDDA: Then you have left your home – for good and all?

THEA: Yes. There was nothing else to be done.

Act 1

Sleepova
Matilda Feyişayọ Ibini

Shan (Nigerian and Jamaican heritage) and Funmi (Nigerian heritage) are friends who, alongside the remainder of their friendship group, see their sleepovas as a place of fun, gossip and honesty. In this scene, Shan and Funmi are in Funmi's bedroom. Funmi's father is dead, and Shan lives with sickle cell. They try to understand each other's experiences.

(*Shan rushes to hug an unreceptive Funmi. Shan hugs her for quite a long while. Shan picks up an empty glass bottle from the dresser.*)

SHAN: Not you sipping on the Jesus juice.

FUNMI: It's Shloer. Rey was right, it can't get you drunk.

SHAN: You look good, can I say that? Honestly you do, your skin's glowing, you're looking extra thick in all the right places –

FUNMI: – Shan, my dad's died, I've not had a BBL. These compliments, *oti poju*, it's too much fam.

SHAN: Sorry, I just... I don't know what to say.

FUNMI: You don't have to say anything.

(*They sit in a heavy silence.*)

(*Shan opens her water bottle and takes a few sips. Shan slips a tablet into her mouth and then drinks some more water. They look around the room before making eye contact at each other. They smile then look away.*)

FUNMI: My brother won't stop calling my dad's phone to hear his voice. And my sister, I don't know where she went, probably gone to be with her not-so-secret boyfriend. Mum's panicking a bit, turns out it's expensive to die on the weekend. My dad's family in Nigeria are talking about, they want him buried over there and my mum's like but who's gon pay for that?

SHAN: Is there anything we can do? I don't know much about funerals.

FUNMI: People die. You bury them. It's natural innit. My dad says, when he dies he'll haunt me and my siblings gently. I told him to leave money everywhere so I'll know it's him. If you find any, it's mine.

SHAN: I believe you will see him again, ain't that right?

(*Beat.*)

SHAN: So how did he die?

FUNMI: I don't know what caused it. It's not like he was sick, or on any medication or anything.

(*Beat.*)

Obviously I was getting ready for our link up to see Black Panther, when my mum came in and asked me to take a seat. (*Tries not to laugh.*) And I'm thinking can you not see that I'm already sat down trying to do my eyeliner. Then she said dad's colleagues found him... I was really looking forward to this since seeing the trailer and we haven't linked up in a while but by the time I got to my door I realised I couldn't come. Is that bad? That I really wanted to come anyway... The film starts in an hour, you can still make it if you leave now. I heard Letitia Wright was going to drop by.

SHAN: Don't be silly, not going anywhere. Wakanda can wait. (*Crosses her arms, doing the Wakanda Forever salute.*) Fortuanta fruits forever!

(*Beat.*)

FUNMI: What's poppin' in Shanland?

SHAN: I'm seeing this new guy Malachi. We met at McDonald's. He works there and he gave me a free McFlurry.

FUNMI: Couldn't he give you a free burger? Cheapskate.

SHAN: I like him, and he knows about my sickle cell. His nan has dementia so he's used to being around sick people. We just celebrated our three-month anniversary, I've not had a crisis since we met. He told me I was the type of girl

he'd been looking for even though he doesn't usually date brunettes. He even said he wants to introduce me to his family.

(*Shan reveals a picture of him on her phone.*)

SHAN: That's Malachi.

FUNMI: *E gba mi o.* This boy is white.

SHAN: And...?

FUNMI: But you said his name was Malachi.

SHAN: There are white people called Malachi. It's in the Bible.

FUNMI: You know white boys. He can kill you, chop you up and feed you to his dog. Do you want to become a documentary?

SHAN: He doesn't have a dog – he's got a cat.

FUNMI: So you want to become cat food?

SHAN: Don't start with all that, you should only date black boys –

FUNMI: – White boys grow up into white men.

SHAN: Who don't get sickle cell or pass on the trait.

FUNMI: Are you dating my man for his blood?

SHAN: I'm not a vampire. My life isn't a joke. I have to think about my future every day – whether I'll have kids of not, when do I check if my boyfriend has the trait, do I get him to do a blood test on the first date? Will I even live long enough to start a family? This drove my dad away, it scared off Marcus –

FUNMI: – You will live long.

SHAN: You don't know that. Every crisis is just that. A crisis – because I don't know if I will survive it. I can be in so much pain my body just shuts down, I pass out and I don't know if I'll wake up. Like I don't feel safe when I'm alone, what if I can't reach my phone in time or I can't get to A&E in time, is this it for me?

(*Beat.*)

FUNMI: I didn't know that's how bad it gets.

SHAN: There's always this assumption that you'll see me again. It's hard not to feel like I'm running out of time.

Scene 8

Glossary: Yoruba word (translation/explanation in English)
Oti poju (it's too much)
E gba mi o (help me [to understand])

The Great Gatsby

F. Scott Fitzgerald, adapted by LAMDA

Tom and Gatsby are at the Plaza Hotel. It is a scorching hot day. Gatsby is a mysterious figure who is in love with Tom's wife Daisy. In this scene, Tom decides to quiz Gatsby about his life, which escalates into an argument over Daisy.

TOM: Mr Gatsby, I understand you're an Oxford man.

GATSBY: Not exactly.

TOM: Oh, yes, I understand you went to Oxford.

GATSBY: Yes – I went there.

TOM: You must have gone there about the same time Biloxi went to New Haven.

GATSBY: I told you I went there.

TOM: I heard you, but I'd like to know when.

GATSBY: It was in nineteen-nineteen, I only stayed five months. That's why I can't really call myself an Oxford man. It was an opportunity they gave to some of the officers after the armistice. We could go to any of the universities in England or France.

TOM: I want to ask you one more question.

GATSBY: Go on.

TOM: What kind of row are you trying to cause in my house anyhow?

(Beat.)

I suppose the latest thing is to sit back and let Mr Nobody from Nowhere take your wife. Well, if that's the idea you can count me out.

GATSBY: I've got something to tell *you*, old sport –

TOM: That's a great expression of yours, isn't it?

GATSBY: Your wife doesn't love you. She's never loved you. She loves me.

TOM: You must be crazy!

GATSBY: She never loved you, do you hear? She only married you because I was poor and she was tired of waiting for me. It was a terrible mistake, but in her heart she never loved anyone except me. Going on for five years – and you didn't know. Both of us loved each other all that time, old sport, and you didn't know. I used to laugh sometimes to think that you didn't know.

TOM: You're crazy! I can't speak about what happened five years ago, because I didn't know Daisy then – and I'll be damned if I see how you got within a mile of her unless you brought the groceries to the back door. But all the rest of that's a God damned lie. Daisy loved me when she was married and she loves me now.

GATSBY: No.

TOM: She does, though. The trouble is that sometimes she gets foolish ideas in her head and doesn't know what she's doing. And what's more, I love Daisy too. Once in a while I go off on a spree and make a fool of myself, but I always come back, and in my heart I love her all the time. I'm going to take better care of her from now on.

GATSBY: You don't understand. You're not going to take care of her anymore.

TOM: I'm not? Why's that?

GATSBY: Daisy's leaving you.

TOM: Nonsense. She's not leaving me! Certainly not for some common swindler who'd have to steal the ring he put on her finger. Who are you, anyhow? You're one of that bunch that hangs around with Meyer Wolfshiem – that much I happen to know. I've made a little investigation into your affairs – and I'll carry it further tomorrow.

GATSBY: You can suit yourself about that, old sport.

TOM: I found out what your 'drugstores' were. He and this Wolfshiem bought up a lot of side-street drugstores here and in Chicago and sold grain alcohol over the counter. That's one of his little stunts. I picked him for a bootlegger the first time I saw him, and I wasn't far wrong.

GATSBY: What about it? I guess your friend Walter Chase wasn't too proud to come in on it.

TOM: And you left him in the lurch, didn't you? You let him go to jail for a month over in New Jersey. God! You ought to hear Walter on the subject of you.

GATSBY: He came to us dead broke. He was very glad to pick up some money, old sport.

TOM: Don't you call me 'old sport!' Walter could have you up on the betting laws too, but Wolfshiem scared him into shutting his mouth. That drug-store business was just small change, but you've got something on now that Walter's afraid to tell me about.

(*Gatsby freezes. Long pause.*)

TOM: You start on home, Daisy. In Mr Gatsby's car. Go on. He won't annoy you. I think he realizes that his presumptuous little flirtation is over.

Chapter 7

Emilia

Morgan Lloyd Malcolm

Emilia1, a character inspired by the poet Emilia Bassano, has just married Alphonso Lanier. They are about to celebrate their marriage when Lanier takes himself off to celebrate with his friends. Left alone, Emilia is frustrated and does not know what to do or where to go. Then, Shakespeare appears and tries to woo her.

SHAKESPEARE: When we met the first time I didn't have a chance to properly introduce myself but I was taken by your charm.

EMILIA1: You liked my face you mean.

SHAKESPEARE: Yes

EMILIA1: My skin.

SHAKESPEARE: Yes.

EMILIA1: You find me intriguing perhaps? You find me a 'breath of fresh air'. You find me exciting maybe. You want to give me a try. You want to see whether things are different with me. You want to even perhaps rescue me. Perhaps you want to sweep me off and coddle me. Protect me. Perhaps you want to sympathise with me. Pity me. Be my champion. Encourage me. Step into the heroes shoes and alter my fate. Is that it? Because I've heard all of this before. A thousand times from all the men who skulk past and sniff at me like dogs. I don't care who you are but you will not be able to say or give me anything I have not had before. And besides, I'm married now. You should find someone better suited to your attentions.

(She goes to leave.)

SHAKESPEARE: You're so angry. Why? You're like a trapped wasp.

EMILIA1: Alright. We're doing this are we?

SHAKESPEARE: Doing what?

EMILIA1: You know what. Fine. Let's do it. If I am a wasp, best beware my sting.

SHAKESPEARE: If you sting me I'll pluck it out.

EMILIA1: Ay if you can find it.

SHAKESPEARE: Who doesn't know where a wasp keeps his sting? It's in his tail!

EMILIA1: In his tongue.

SHAKESPEARE: Who's tongue?

EMILIA1: Your tongue if you don't leave me be.

SHAKESPEARE: Is this... I mean... are we? I don't know what this is.

EMILIA1: I do know of you, you know. How can I not? I hear you are a poet.

SHAKESPEARE: I am.

EMILIA1: Me too.

SHAKESPEARE: You write?

EMILIA1: I do.

(*They circle each other. They're wooing each other.*)

SHAKESPEARE: How oft, when thou, my music, music play'st,
Upon that blessed wood whose motion sounds
With thy sweet fingers, when thou gently sway'st
The wiry concord that mine ear confounds,
Do I envy those jacks that nimble leap
To kiss the tender inward of thy hand,
Whilst my poor lips, which should that harvest reap
At the wood's boldness by thee blushing stand!
To be so tickled, they would change their state
And situation with those dancing chips,
O'er whom thy fingers walk with gentle gait,
Making dead wood more blest than living lips.

Since saucy jacks so happy are in this,
Give them thy fingers, me thy lips to kiss.

(*At some point over the following Shakespeare gives her a rose.*)

EMILIA1: How I would make him fawn, and beg, and seek,
And wait the season, and observe the time,
And spend his prodigal wits in bootless rhymes,
And shape his service wholly to my hests,
And make him proud to make me proud that jests!
So pertaunt like would I o'ersway his state
That he should be my fool, and I his fate.

(*She gives the rose to someone in the audience. Shakespeare reacts angrily. Over the following Emilia1 reacts to his insults.*)

SHAKESPEARE: My mistress' eyes are nothing like the sun;
Coral is far more red than her lips' red:
If snow be white, why then her breasts are dun;
If hairs be wires, black wires grow on her head.

EMILIA1: That's racist!

SHAKESPEARE: I have seen roses damask'd, red and white,
But no such roses see I in her cheeks;
And in some perfumes is there more delight
Than in the breath that from my mistress reeks.
I love to hear her speak, yet well I know
That music hath a far more pleasing sound:
I grant I never saw a goddess go;
My mistress, when she walks, treads on the ground.
And yet, by heaven, I think my love as rare
As any she belied with false compare

EMILIA1: Come, gentle night, come, loving, black-brow'd night,
Give me my Will, and, when I shall die,
Take him and cut him out in little stars,
And he will make the face of heaven so fine

That all the world will be in love with night,
And pay no worship to the garish sun.

Act 1, Scene 5

Treasure Island

Bryony Lavery, adapted from the novel by **Robert Louis Stevenson**

Jim is on the hunt for treasure. Jim was previously on board a ship with Captain Long John Silver, who turned out to be a traitor looking to steal all the money. Having recently escaped Captain Long John Silver with the treasure map, Jim washes up on Billy Bones' Island. In this scene, Jim meets Ben Gunn, a cabin boy who was also betrayed by Captain Long John Silver.

(*Another part of the island...*
Jim drops from somewhere hidden...
She is dripping wet, exhausted and in a very bad mood.)

JIM: Something's... glooping!!!!!

(*Something is glooping!!!*)

Oh... Grandma!!!!

(*She approaches the glooping... A strange swamplike creature pops up from the ground in front of her...*)

Aaaagh!!!

BEN GUNN: *Aaagh!!!!*

(*They stare at each other in unabashed horror.*)

JIM: *What are You????*

BEN GUNN: Ip ip ip ip

JIM: Are you *human???????*

BEN GUNN: Nnnnn sh ... (*Not sure any more.*)
I'm Ben Gunn I haven't spoken to any one but myself these past three years
THREE YEARS!!!!! haven't you Ben Gunn????
What Ben Gunn SPEAKUP!!!!! Spoken to anyone but yourself these past three years? No NO!!!!! I haven't so you're ... Ben Gunn????
I am are you yes I am YES I AM!!!!

(*Stares more.*)

What are you????

(*Nips her.*)

JIM: Ouch NO!!!! Why did you nip me?

BEN GUNN: See if you is real or product of my probably now diseased brain!

JIM: Yes I is real!!!!

BEN GUNN: Mightn't have a bit of cheese about you?

(*Ben Gunn searches Jim for cheese...*)

JIM: Don't do that

BEN GUNN: I haven't had cheese not real cheese for three years

JIM: I'm serious don't do that

BEN GUNN: I've had cheese of the diseased imagination but it's not the same as real cheese

(*Jim tries to unclamp Ben Gunn's searching hands...*)

Real *Toasted* cheese

JIM: Stop searching me Ben Gunn or / I will

BEN GUNN: That ship out there ... Is that a real ship if so what ship name quick name quick name quick!!!!

(*Nips her.*)

JIM: Why don't you swim out and nip it... find out for yourself????

BEN GUNN: Ben Gunn can't swim.
Ben Gunn has dreamed of a real ship almost more
   than he's dreamed of cheese.
Ben Gunn wishes he could get on that ship and sail
   HOME don't you Ben Gunn?

Oh yes to a SAFE WARM PLACE with more than
ME some GOOD humans and Real CHEESE
    TOASTED for PREFERENCE!!!!
    Is that your ship?

JIM: Yes!

BEN GUNN: Wwwwwwwwwwwwwwwwwwwwwone-llllllegged
    man on it at all??????

JIM: Yes!

BEN GUNN: Ssssssssssssssssssssssssil vvvvvvvvvvvver...???????

JIM: Yes!
You know Long John Silver????

BEN GUNN: Ip ip

(*In immense dread, Ben Gunn loses power of breathing.*)

JIM: How do you know Long John Silver???
How????
Speak!

BEN GUNN: Ip

JIM: You're soooo thin...!!!! scrawny almost... you're
    the cabin boy the scrawny cabin boy!!!!!

BEN GUNN: Ip ip ip

JIM: Just nod

(*Ben Gunn nods.*)

On the *Walrus*!!!????

Just nod!

(*Ben Gunn nods.*)

They left you on the island?

(*Nods.*)

Why?
Were you bad?
Did they just forget you?
I'm a Pirate-Fighter you need to tell me...

(*Ben Gunn can't speak.*)

Ben Gunn if you can get some words out... I'll put
   you on my ship
And feed you cheese...

BEN GUNN: Silver says CaptainFlintwants sixreliableswabstobury
   yourtreasureonthisherehandyisland.
 He says I picked already
 AllardyceO'DohertyMcGrawThimbleGiantGrimes
 Who for the sixth?
 Silver says 'Captain Flint, take Ben Gunn along of you
   forheistheonlywritingPersononboardship sohecan
   write thecluesfortherefinding oftreasureandheis
   smart as paint.'

JIM: He said that to *me*!

BEN GUNN: And looked out for *you too*?

JIM: Right up until the time he *didn't*

BEN GUNN: Right up until the time he *didn't*!!!!

JIM: Ben Gunn. I *swear* on a lump of the *tastiest* cheese
   I will be your true friend
We are both smart as paint, with four legs between
   us and two ... one and a half good brains!
We will defy and defeat our one-legged nightmare!

Act 2, 'Wet Jim Meets The Monster'

Title Index

Author Index

Copyright and Acknowledgements

Christou, Georgia, *Bright. Young. Things.** © 2020 Georgia Christou. Reproduced by permission of Nick Hern Books.

Churchill, Caryl, *Love and Information** © 2012 Caryl Churchill. Reproduced by permission of Nick Hern Books.

Cole, Curtis, *Sherbet* © 2024 Curtis Cole. Reproduced by permission of the author and The Agency (London) Limited.

Cooke, Trish, *A Husband for Mum, The Letter, Ella and Buttons Make Their Own Party* and *Little Red and Big Blue's Deal* © 2024 Trish Cooke. Reproduced by permission of the author.

Dockrill, Laura, *Robin Hood** © 2018 Laura Dockrill. Reproduced by permission of United Agents.

Edmundson, Helen, *Coram Boy** © 2005 Helen Edmundson, adapted from the novel by Jamila Gavin. Reproduced by permission of Nick Hern Books.

Green, JJ, *A-Typical Rainbow** © 2022 JJ Green. Reproduced by permission of Nick Hern Books.

Gupta, Tanika, *Anita and Me** © Tanika Gupta, adapted from the novel by Meera Syal, 2021, *Anita and Me*, Methuen Drama, an imprint of Bloomsbury Publishing Plc. Reproduced by permission of Bloomsbury Publishing Plc.

Gupta, Tanika and **Kay, Jackie**, *Red Dust Road* © Tanika Gupta and Jackie Kay, 2019, *Red Dust Road*, Methuen Drama, an imprint of Bloomsbury Publishing Plc. Reproduced by permission of Bloomsbury Publishing Plc.

Hesmondhalgh, Rosa, *Cheese and Pickle, The Skin You're In, Like Lennon* and *Twitch* © 2024 Rosa Hesmondhalgh. Reproduced by permission of the author.

Hickson, Ella, *Wendy & Peter Pan** © 2015 Ella Hickson, adapted from the novel by J. M. Barrie. Reproduced by permission of Nick Hern Books.

Ibini, Matilda Feyiṣayọ, *Sleepova** © 2023 Matilda Feyiṣayọ Ibini. Reproduced by permission of Matilda Feyiṣayọ Ibini and Independent Talent.

Kabuya, Allegresse, with **Glasier, Ned, Greenaway-Bailey, Sadeysa**, and **Company Three**, *When This Is Over** © 2023 Ned Glasier, Sadeysa Greenaway-Bailey and Company Three. Reproduced by permission of Nick Hern Books.

Kennedy, Fin, *Fast** © 2015 Fin Kennedy. Reproduced by permission of Nick Hern Books.

Kennedy, Hannah, *This Massive Universe, A Monster Called Hex, Flicker* and *Proud* © 2024 Hannah Kennedy. Reproduced by permission of the author.

Khalil, Hannah, *The Fir Tree** © Hannah Khalil, 2022, *The Fir Tree*, Methuen Drama, an imprint of Bloomsbury Publishing Plc. Reproduced by permission of Bloomsbury Publishing Plc.

Lane, David, *Off the Grid* © 2024 David Lane, commissioned by Half Moon Theatre. Reproduced by permission of the author.

Lavery, Bryony, *Treasure Island** written by Robert Louis Stevenson and adapted by Bryony Lavery. Reproduced by permission of United Agents.

Lavery, Bryony, *The Book of Dust – La Belle Sauvage** © 2021 Bryony Lavery, adapted from the novel by Philip Pullman. Reproduced by permission of Nick Hern Books.

Lavery, Hannah, *The Raven** © 2022 Hannah Lavery. Reproduced by permission of the author.

Lewis, Henry, Shields, Henry and **Sayer, Jonathan**, *Peter Pan Goes Wrong** © Henry Lewis, Henry Shields, Jonathan Sayer, 2015, *Peter Pan Goes Wrong*, Methuen Drama, an imprint of Bloomsbury Publishing Plc. Reproduced by permission of Bloomsbury Publishing Plc.

MacRae, Tom, *Everybody's Talking About Jamie: Teen Edition** © 2022 Tom MacRae. Reproduced by permission of the author and The Agency (London) Limited.

Madge, Rob, *My Son's A Queer (But What Can You Do?)** © 2021 Rob Madge. Reproduced by permission of Nick Hern Books.

Mahfouz, Sabrina, *Noughts & Crosses* © 2020 Sabrina Mahfouz, adapted from the novel by Malorie Blackman. Reproduced by permission of Nick Hern Books.

Mahfouz, Sabrina and **McNish, Holly**, *Offside** © Sabrina Mahfouz and Hollie McNish, 2017, *Offside*, Methuen Drama, an imprint of Bloomsbury Publishing Plc. Reproduced by permission of Bloomsbury Publishing Plc.

Malcolm, Morgan Lloyd, *Emilia** © Morgan Lloyd Malcolm, 2021, *Emilia*, Methuen Drama, an imprint of Bloomsbury Publishing Plc. Reproduced by permission of Bloomsbury Publishing Plc.

Poltergeist Theatre, *Alice in Wonderland* © 2022 Jack Bradfield, Gerel Falconer and Poltergeist Theatre. Reproduced by permission of Independent Talent and Esta Charkham Associates.

Raczka, Lulu, *Antigone** © Lulu Raczka, 2021, *Antigone*, Methuen Drama, an imprint of Bloomsbury Publishing Plc. Reproduced by permission of Bloomsbury Publishing Plc.

Razia, Ambreen, *The Diary of a Hounslow Girl** © 2016 Ambreen Razia. Reproduced by permission of Aurora Metro Books (www.aurorametro.com).

Reiss, Anya, *Oliver Twist* © Anya Reiss, adapted from the novel by Charles Dickens, 2017, *Oliver Twist*, Methuen Drama, an imprint of Bloomsbury Publishing Plc. Reproduced by permission of Bloomsbury Publishing Plc.

Shakespeare, William, *Hamlet*, King Henry V*, A Midsummer Night's Dream*, The Tempest*, The Two Gentlemen of Verona* and *Twelfth Night,* from *Arden Shakespeare Complete Works* © edited by Ann Thompson, David Scott Kastan, Richard Proudfoot, 2011, Arden Shakespeare Complete Works, an imprint of Bloomsbury Publishing Plc. Reproduced by permission of Bloomsbury Publishing Plc.

Shakthidharan, S., *The Bone Sparrow* © 2022 S. Shakthidharan, adapted from the novel by Zana Fraillon. Reproduced by permission of Nick Hern Books.

Stephens, Simon, *The Curious Incident of the Dog in the Night-Time** © Simon Stephens, adapted from the novel by Mark Haddon, 2012, *The Curious Incident of the Dog in the Night-Time*, Methuen Drama, an imprint of Bloomsbury Publishing Plc. Reproduced by permission of Bloomsbury Publishing Plc.

Teed, Nick, *It Makes You Wonder* © 2023 Nick Teed. Reproduced by permission of the author.

Thorne, Jack, *Hamish** from *CripTales: Six Monologues* © 2020 Jack Thorne. Reproduced by permission of Nick Hern Books.

Virk, Manjinder, *Glow** © 2003 Manjinder Virk. Reproduced by permission of Aurora Metro Books (www.aurorametro.com).

Webster, Bea, *Is This A Fairytale?** © 2020 Bea Webster. Reproduced by permission of Brennan Artists on behalf of the author.

Williams, Tyrell, *Red Pitch** © 2022 Tyrell Williams. Reproduced by permission of Nick Hern Books.